Because the decision to get married is one of the most important in life, you know that it requires careful consideration. In *Before Saying "I Do,"* James L. Christensen offers straightforward counsel, from a Christian perspective, for all who consider marriage. His realistic approach will allow you to honestly evaluate your relationship, meet difficulties constructively, and make necessary adjustments before the wedding, thereby building a secure foundation for marriage. A reflection guide at the beginning of each chapter will stimulate your thoughts and provide relevant questions that need to be discussed. Through the guidance shared here, you'll add a new dimension to your love and be assured that each of you understands the seriousness of the marriage commitment.

By James L. Christensen

Funeral Services
The Minister's Service Handbook
The Minister's Marriage Handbook
The Complete Funeral Manual
Contemporary Worship Services
Funeral Services for Today
The Minister's Church, Home, and
     Community Services Handbook
Before Saying "I Do"

Before Saying "I Do"

James L. Christensen

Power Books

Fleming H. Revell Company
Old Tappan, New Jersey

Scripture quotations in this volume are from the Revised Standard Version of the Bible, copyrighted 1946, 1952, © 1971 and 1973.

Marry the Man Today by Frank Loesser from "Guys and Dolls" © 1950 FRANK MUSIC Corp.

International Copyright Secured All Rights Reserved Used By Permission.

Material from YOUR WEDDING WORK BOOK—Belting & Hine, Interstate Publishers, Danville, Illinois. Used with permission from the authors.

Quotation from DEAR ABBY copyright, 1983, Universal Press Syndicate. Reprinted with permission. All rights reserved. (Taken from the DEAR ABBY column).

Material reprinted from *Pre-Marital Counseling Guide,* by permission of Fortress Press.

Marriage Laws Chart from Reader's Digest FAMILY LEGAL GUIDE. Copyright © 1981 by The Reader's Digest Association, Inc. Used by permission.

Library of Congress Cataloging in Publication Data

Christensen, James L.
  Before saying "I do"

  "Power books."
  1. Love.   2. Mate selection.   3. Marriage.   4. Marriage—Religious aspects—Christianity.   I. Title.
HQ801.C487   1983   646.77   83-9517
ISBN 0-8007-5128-0

TO
Dr. Charles (Chuck) Kemp
a friend of many years
and
trusted counselor to our family

Contents

Preface

Happy and enduring marriages are achieved as a result of the most mature and conscious effort of which human beings are capable. Couples have to work at building a worthy relationship. If you succeed in your marriage, you will have climbed one of the highest and most difficult mountains on the human scene.

Most persons who marry believe their marriage will be blissful and divorce proof. Fifty percent or more are disappointed. The city in which I live has one of the highest divorce ratios in the nation. Divorce contradicts all a husband and wife profess when they exchange their vows. It ultimately negates their earlier shared feelings of love and respect.

It has become my obsession to do something constructive to reverse the prevailing divorce epidemic. Part of the solution lies in more thorough preparation for marriage. Tightening up the entrance exams should decrease the easy exits. Enduring marriage is possible!

This book is designed for couples contemplating marriage to read and discuss early in their courtship.

Blessed is the happily married couple. They are like two trees that, though separated by their planting, grow tall and straight, stretching toward the sun. As they reach out, the distance between them decreases. They become increasingly aware of each other as their branches overlap and their roots intertwine. Together they sway in the wind, sing in the sun, and dance in the breeze. Through the years, nurtured by common soil, they stand strong, side by side, protecting each other in the storms, enjoying the beauty of God's earth, and serving His purposes for them. Saplings spring up in their shadows and grow strong and independent, ready to take over when age and infirmity overcome the perennials. Cut deeply in the bark of each, which time can never efface, will be the tender words, "I love you."

So may it be with you, dear readers.

Reflection Guide 1

1. Why do you want to marry? Are these worthy reasons?
2. Can you fulfill God's purpose for your life better single or married? in what ways?
3. Are you enthusiastic about marriage?
4. What benefits do you see in marriage?
5. What are the responsibilities in marriage?
6. Are you willing to assume the responsibilities?
7. Do you know without any doubts or hesitation that this is what you want to do?
8. Is there a total inward concurrence that this is right for both of you?
9. Have you sought counsel from your parents, pastor, or friends?
10. Have you prayed for guidance?

1

Do You Really Want to Marry?

Right to Be Single

You have a legitimate right not to marry, if you desire. Though the Bible approves a person leaving father and mother to become united in marriage, it also conveys the right of human freedom in this regard. Marriage was ordained of God, approved by Jesus of Nazareth, and commended by the Apostle Paul as part of God's creation, yet Jesus commended the unmarried (Matthew 19:10-12), and the Apostle Paul did likewise (1 Corinthians 7:8), conveying that there are vocations best accomplished by a single person. The Roman Catholic Church has for centuries required its priests and nuns to remain celibate, a position to which Protestant and Orthodox churches do not adhere, nor does Judaism make such a claim for its rabbis.

Some people remain single because they are not fortunate enough to find the kind of mates they wish to live with all their lives. They prepare to make life meaningful, whether or not they marry. If the right relationship develops, they will marry, but do not wish to compromise just to be married. Because of the imbalance of women and men in the United States, it means many more single people will never have a chance to marry.

Other Reasons for Remaining Single

Many youths today, however, have chosen to remain single for less worthy reasons. Perhaps one-third of the young people in America feel marriage is obsolete. They may fear the stereotypes and restrictions of marriage. They may want to retain the freedom and flexibility of singleness. They may choose a career as more satisfying and less complicated than marriage. Since sex pleasures are so easily available in our sensual society, they may not wish the added burdens of marriage, when the sex drives can be satisfied without commitment. Some choose a homosexual life-style, which does not fit the marriage pattern. Some singles today have been married but were "burned" with an unhappy experience. As one has said, "I would rather be single and wish that I were married than to be married and wish that I were single again."

Should I Marry?

People marry for a variety of reasons—some good, some bad. Some marry for inadequate reasons, contributing to the inevitable breakup of the union. At the outset test your motives objectively and honestly.

Wrong Reasons for Marriage

ESCAPE Some people marry to escape an intolerable home situation. They wish to get away from the authority of a judgmental, restrictive father; or from the temper, outbursts, and domination of a possessive mother; or from unbearable conflicts, noise, and clutter; or from poverty. Some are treated as children by their parents, in spite of their age, so they wish to get away from what they consider irrational and unnecessary treatment, however well intentioned. Some marry to escape boredom and loneliness or the responsibility of being the breadwinner. Others marry to escape insecurity—financially and emotionally.

Are you wishing to marry so you can escape an unhappy home situation? If so, it is hardly an adequate basis for entering marriage.

MONEY   A recent news release indicates that more and more women are making money their number-one qualification in a husband. This is the money generation. "Marrying money, a subject once considered too gauche to mention in public, now is not only talked about but taught. In fact, prospecting gold-diggers around the country are flocking to self-improvement courses to learn the best methods of finding and capturing monied mates." As one lady said, "It's not that hard to meet men with money. It's getting them to propose that takes work." Another confides, "The way to wealth has many shortcuts. These days, though, the heavy traffic is in lover's lane."[1]

LEGITIMIZE SEX   Others marry to legitimize the sexual lusts in which they have indulged, some to legitimize a child whom they have conceived or born out of wedlock.

Frequently, when pregnancy becomes known, the girl or her parents demand the couple marry to save embarrassment or to "give the child" a legitimate name. If such a couple is not truly in love, well matched, or adequately prepared for marriage, such an action can be tragic. Two wrongs never make a right. Much better for the girl to go to a maternity home for unwed mothers, have the baby, place it for adoption, then continue her education and employment until she can overcome the emotional scars and perhaps marry later with nobler motives and more mature judgment.

BEING PUSHED   Some people, especially among the young, but not exclusively, find themselves pushed into marriage by their friends or family. Others call them a "perfect couple," just right for each other. Single people are teased by thoughtless friends and constantly "set up" with introductions or blind dates. Society exerts inordinate pressures, subtle and overt, upon single persons in an attempt to alter their unmarried status. Often the date puts on the pressure.

A single minister friend left the ministry because, he admitted, the parents of single ladies forever tried to match him with their daughters; church leaders and members always strove to set him up; he was teased privately and publicly about being single. "I just couldn't take it any longer," he confessed.

Face the questions outright: Are you doing this voluntarily, because you want to? Are you being pushed by your friends, by your mother or father? Does either of you feel trapped? Would you like to be out of it, but do not want to injure others? It is better to endure the pain of separation now than later! You'll find it better to uncover an unworthy motive for marriage before discovering its entanglements!

COMPANIONSHIP   The decline of religious sanctions in marriage and the diminished role of religious practices in life have led to a different view of marriage. Marriage today is considered more a matter of companionship than a commitment sanctified by law and society. The general secularization of life, which denies the transcendent divine dimension, has made it easier to enter marriage with little or no required preparation and equally easy to abandon it with little of the social stigma once experienced by those who were divorced. The stance of most churches regarding divorce has softened. Marriages may involve the "solemnization" by a clergyman, yet by and large, the religious influence goes little beyond that. So it has been commonplace for people to go in and out of marriage with little hesitancy, depending upon the whim of the moment. This throw-away society advocates the fashion of discarding wives and husbands with the same reckless abandon with which one rids oneself of a used-up car or a faded, aging garment.

RESPONSIBLE SEX Marriage gives the framework for beautiful, responsible sex with love and commitment. So marrying for the enjoyment of sex is legitimate if love accompanies this motive. This natural God-given drive for the pleasure of a man and a woman and for the procreation of the human race demands the security of commitment. Sex expresses the true erotic love of a man for a woman and a woman for a man. Love without sex is but partial. Sex without love is lust. Sex without love or commitment is sinful.

Marriage gives the security where sex can be legitimately done within a continuing, acknowledged commitment; it provides the social structure for the giving of oneself in love, with complete abandonment. Your desire to share your love in sex with the continuing commitment of responsibility is a good reason to get married. You have God's blessing!

Yet a happy and enduring marriage requires more factors than biological functioning.

Deeper Reasons for Marriage

FEEL GOD'S WILL Why then should you marry? The decision should be made from the perspective of God's will. Do you believe God wants you to share your life with another person in marriage? Will you be able to use your God-given talents in this marriage? Will it allow you to love and trust and serve God, or will it handicap such a devotion? Does your desire for marriage reflect the finest aspiration and desires in you? Or does it appeal to your more selfish and ugly moods and instincts? Can this marriage have any relation to God at all?

How can you best serve the purposes of God for your life? He gives you freedom to decide. Your family's expectations or society's conventions alone should not determine your course. You make the decision, according to your view of God's will for your life, believing that God's blessings are bestowed upon the single and married indiscriminately and that you fulfill purposes in life either way.

NOT AN IDOL   The Christian community has never maintained that marriage is the ultimate goal in human life, the end-all of existence. The Bible describes marriage as a merciful gift from God (1 Corinthians 7:7–9), yet Jesus taught that the demands of God should always take precedence over the demands of marriage (Luke 14:20, 26) and family (Mark 3:31–35; Matthew 10:37). The ultimate meaning of life centers in our relationship with Jesus Christ. Each individual has a useful identity, unique talents, and special opportunities to serve God. The first commandment: "You shall have no other gods before me" (Exodus 20:3) indicates that matrimony cannot finally fulfill all our needs, goals, and desires. God alone can fill those places.

FULFILL LIFE'S PURPOSES   Christ calls us to a life of responsibility and trust. Most people find that marriage best teaches them to become responsible persons and to live in trust.

We are called to a life of love and forgiveness. In truth, the intimacy of marriage most often nearly approximates the perfect love Christ demonstrated for us. Our love is never perfect in this world, but in relation to our mates and our children, we far exceed what we experience in other relationships. Our forgiveness is always partial, yet we most forgive those loved persons around our table, who have so often forgiven us.

Christ calls us to a life of purposeful service. We can most readily see meaning in life and purpose to existence, in the roles as marriage partners and as parents.

If you have a mate whom you truly love, who shares these high motives, and will become your partner in living out God's will with you, then it is okay to marry.

sure, self-fulfillment, and growth. The O'Neills' description makes it deceptively attractive and tempting.

However, there is a convincing case for monogamous marriage and fidelity within it. Many marital counselors disagree with the concept of open marriage. All Christians should. "Most sexually mature adults do not enjoy being adulterers," asserts Dr. George R. Bach, director of the Institute for Group Psychotherapy in Beverly Hills, California. "For real intimates, infidelity tends to pall."[2]

Those who think they can be faithful to another in soul, but unfaithful in body, forget that the two are inseparable. Sex in isolation from personality does not exist. A person has no organic functions isolated from his soul.

Sex apart from committed marriage would give hearts emotions, but no homes; would give birds flights, but no nests; would launch a voyager to sea, but with no port. Monogamous marriage provides the home, the nest, the port for intimacy.

Monogamous marriage is a dependable structure, based on mutual commitment to each other, a necessity for personality growth as created by God. We need intimacy; we need love; we need opportunity to give and to be needed; we need recognition for what we achieve and are, and acceptance and understanding. We need outlets for the pleasure that our senses and bodies can bring to us; we need to feel worthwhile and worthy. No relation more pleasurably and adequately meets these needs than the committed marriage.

Just think, in the exclusive marriage, there is "only one person in the world toward whom you are totally open and free; only one person from whom there is no concealment, to whom you share all your secrets, whose body is as dear to you, in every part, as your own."[3] Only in the exclusive marriage is there no sense of mine and thine in property or possessions. The streams of two personalities converge and flow together, intertwined, forging out the future path. In the natural flow of oneness there exists the spontaneity of new joys and experiences, with periods of still refreshment, as well as the ripples of shared difficulties and falls of sorrow. From the depths flow the springs of sympathy and renewing grace. Only in the truly committed and exclusive marriage can this be realized.

Reflections Guide 3

1. Do you accept the possibility that you may stay single and never marry again?
2. Are you being pressed to get married again?
3. What is the position of your religion regarding remarriage? Have you reconciled your conscience? From a theological and biblical perspective, do you feel you can marry again?
4. Is your desire to remarry based upon financial needs? loneliness? sexual desires? insecurity? health? welfare of children? love?
5. Are you more mature than before you were married the last time?
6. Have you given yourself enough time to recover your self-esteem and leave behind negative feelings before allowing another relationship to develop? Are you free enough from your former partner to make an intelligent decision to remarry?
7. Can you accept stepchildren?
8. Is the same source of conflict that caused trouble in your former marriage evident in this relationship?
9. Did your present relationship begin as an affair while you were still married?
10. Are you willing to wholeheartedly commit yourself to making your marriage succeed?

3

Marrying Again?

Should you consider remarriage after a divorce or after being widowed? The average divorced man, although on guard and not without scars from a former marriage, wants to find someone with whom to share his life. The average divorced woman, however well adjusted she may be in her career, usually wonders how many years she will still be single or when she might meet Mr. Right. Widowed people, however devoted to their former mates, dislike the painful loneliness and would prefer to be married.

The desire to be married continues, in spite of Margaret Mead's claims that marriage has become an anthropologic curiosity and despite the much filmed and written about alternatives to marriage. Most men and women want to be married.

Some divorced people go in and out of marriage with the same casualness with which one may enter or terminate a job. Marriage is a far more profound and sacred relationship than the choice of one's occupation, though one's work should have a dimension of sacred calling to it as well.

In 1967 Morton Hunt estimated that 85 percent of divorced men and 76 percent of divorced women eventually remarried. Undoubtedly the statistics are higher today.

Every divorced or widowed person faces the question "Should I remarry if the opportunity is afforded?" The complex reasons for remarrying cannot be attributed to a single motivation. Some may desire companionship or to be settled again. Some need to have a special person with whom to share life and fulfill sexual needs. Some want financial security. Others desire a father or mother to help love and care for the children from a former marriage. To some it is a matter of convenience.

Should You Consider Remarriage?

Many sincere Christians have conscience problems at this point, especially if they have been divorced or are contemplating marrying a divorced person.

Religious Scruples and Divorce

The traditional, historic position is, "No. Remarriage for the divorced is always wrong." It is based on Jesus' words, "And I say to you: whoever divorces his wife, except for unchastity, and marries another, commits adultery" (Matthew 19:9).

The New Testament ideal portrays marriage as a permanent union of one man and one woman. To fail to achieve that ideal is to fall short of God's perfection. The ideal must be held up, proclaimed, honored, and cherished as the goal for every marriage.

Nonetheless, we live in an unideal society where people make wrong choices and are often unequally yoked. The union may be so destructive that divorce appears as the lesser of two evils. Divorce becomes an escape hatch, a way out of a marriage that afforded neither person anything but distress and hurt. Though deeply regretted and seldom encouraged, often divorce is an exit ramp available to those who have made unwise choices in selecting mates or who find changes so drastic since marriage that continuing compatibility proves impossible.

People who have failed in marriage are not by that failure

cut off from God and His forgiveness or unable to fulfill His purposes for their lives. No sin is unforgivable by God if one is truly remorseful, humble, and repentant (Matthew 12:31; Mark 3:28). That means even divorce. Some churches assume a judgmental, dogmatic, and self-righteous stance in regard to such victims. Thus they turn many away from counsel and demonstrate little compassion or sensitivity. The church that closes the door to all divorced people seeking remarriage and recovery probably drives them farther from God.

This is not an appeal for a blanket condoning of divorce. Divorce is forever a regretful conclusion. Yet church leaders must empathize with the victims of divorce. The church may give its blessing and approval to those who demonstrate humble repentance and seek remarriage after much time, prayer, and preparation.

A Redeeming Attitude

F. Lofton Hudson expressed a more redeeming attitude regarding remarriage for the divorced:

> If Jesus were here today facing our moral situations, I have no doubt that He would say, "Not only is it right for some to remarry after they have been divorced, it is downright wrong for them to stay single if they have a good opportunity to remarry and feel that they can live a more fulfilling life by entering into another intimate marital relationship. It is not my will for people to live second-rate lives."[4]

"The second marriage can be more valid and meaningful than the first, particularly because the participants are more mature,"[5] concludes Robert Penske, who has developed a program of pastoral care for persons married the second time.

Often remarrying people exhibit more stability and personality development because they are somewhat older. Rarely does rebellion form the basis of such marriages, which are entered by those who have already answered many essential life questions. Knowing what marriage requires, they face fewer surprises. Because they have benefited from insights concerning the first marriage, a second one offers a fresh start, free from old resentments and detrimental images. Parental influence is considerably less. Having experienced the pain of one failure, the couple determines to make it work, even if it means modified behavior and greater unselfishness.

Jim Smoke put it in another way, "Remarriage for some people is an option, for others it is an opportunity. If God is at work in your life, it will be a great opportunity."[6]

If you have experienced divorce more than once, perhaps you should not remarry. Yours is a poor track record. Marrying three or more times only further desecrates the sacredness of marriage and brings hurt to those with whom you have become entangled. A series of marriages entered into with fingers crossed, for personal convenience, is tantamount to polygamy on the installment plan.

Remarrying After the Death of a Spouse

Death frequently ends a highly successful relationship. The bereaved mate reluctantly considers the thought of remarriage, even after years have elapsed. Remarriage may be construed as disrespect for the dead partner.

Some do not believe in remarriage on religious grounds, believing marriage is for eternity. Others marry again without diminishing their love or feelings for their former spouses. They consider life in chapters. Though one chapter has closed, they do not feel obligated to live forever in the past, doomed to a future of loneliness and grief. If sufficient time has elapsed and the right kind of mates are met, they may marry, feeling their former mates would desire their happiness.

To the religiously oriented, inevitably the question about relationships in the hereafter emerges.

WHAT ABOUT MULTIPLE MARRIAGES IN THE HEREAFTER? The Sadducees brought that question to Jesus (Mark

12:18–27). Because they did not believe in the resurrection, the Sadducees wanted to present the matter in the most unfavorable light possible. They cited the case of a woman who had been married to seven brothers, one after another, all of whom had died. Intending to make survival after death ridiculous, they asked, "In the resurrection, whose wife will she be? . . ." Jesus answered, ". . . when they rise from the dead, they neither marry nor are given in marriage, but are like angels in heaven."

This does not mean that there will be no personal relationships in the afterlife, but they will not include the continuation of physical ties: mutual spiritual kinship will form the basis of the relationships. Often we think of sexual or blood ties as our closest relationships. In actuality our most intimate associations are spiritual and psychological. The experience of a deep rapport and genuine love with a mate develops from a spiritual kinship. True love blends the soul, heart, mind, and will. If the soul is absent in a marriage, there will be no abiding relationship beyond death. If a physical attraction forms its basis, love will diminish when the body diminishes. The spiritual bond is stronger than the bond of flesh.

Wait Ample Time

No firm rules guide how long after being widowed or divorced you should wait to remarry. Individuals' needs vary, but generally speaking, it is best to postpone the decision to marry again for several years. Many people rush into hasty second marriages. The waiting time for remarriage has dwindled. In the fifties the average person who remarried had been single for four years. Now 50 percent of divorced men remarry within four or five months; 75 percent of divorced or widowed persons marry within three years of their marriage termination. Nothing creates more resentment and gossip on the part of family and friends than for a widowed person to marry within months of the spouse's death. Controlled, mature, and respectful people usually wait a minimum of a year.

If you wait a considerable time after a former marriage has ended, your chances for remarrying well will greatly improve. You will be less likely to be influenced by unresolved feelings. Your life can settle down. You can better objectify your life, learn about yourself, gain perspective, project your future goals, more clearly analyze your former marriage, and discover your weaknesses and your strengths. Common sense holds more sway over your life.

Healing Grief

Grief follows any separation such as death or divorce and must be dealt with constructively before it can be assimilated. You must face a rash of emotions, including anger, resentment, blame, guilt, paranoia, and hostility before you can think normally. If not handled constructively and brought under control, these emotions can destroy your relationships and certainly ill equip you for marriage. For some, the healing of grief involves a long psychological process; some never accept it; still others, with proper counsel, support, and faith, assimilate the loss and begin carving out new futures.

Entering into a new marriage relationship before resolving these emotions brings undue strain upon the already difficult task of harmoniously blending two personalities.

If, as a divorced person, you still send your former spouse gifts on birthdays, if you still follow what is happening to his or her career and keep track of the persons dated, then do not assume you are ready for another try at marriage. If you spend energy trying to avoid paying child support, use tactics to harass your former partner, and if you are especially glad to know that your social life is going well while the other's social life is in shambles, chances are you are not sufficiently freed from the past to make a new marriage succeed.

Guard Against a Rebound

Approximately 40 percent of second marriages fail. One would expect that persons who have gone through marriage

once would do better the second time. Nearly half make the
same mistake again.

Time acts as a buffer that guards against this tendency.
Unresolved feelings about a former marriage partner can ad-
versely affect your judgment. Loneliness, fear of insecurity,
feelings of being rejected, guilt for instigating the divorce, desire for companionship—all may propel you blindly into another marriage. When one partner remarries, the other experiences the temptation, as a matter of pride or revenge, to follow
suit.

Ponder Lessons From Your Previous Marriage

Letting time elapse can be a great advantage for persons
contemplating remarriage. You may involve yourself in
lengthy analyses, sharing your experiences and feelings with a
professional therapist who can help objectify your life. You
have a chance to evaluate accurately and seriously what went
wrong in your marriage, to determine the kind of person you
have been and what you did that you should not do in another
marriage relationship.

In a divorce situation, seldom can blame fall totally on one
side. Realize what your contributions were to your first marriage's failure and learn to minimize these in another marriage.
Rethink what has been counterfeit and what has been real.
Given space, stripped of the marriage structure and responsibility, you have time to think and act creatively. You can
project goals for your future and begin remaking your life.
Piece together a sound picture of your potential in marriage.
Thus, a disaster can become your opportunity.

Choose With Care

The basic reason for second marriages failing is the same
reason for first-marriage failure: a poorly made selection of a
marriage mate.

Some people remarry someone whom they see in reference

to the former husband or wife: a person quite similar or one who represents the opposite extreme. This is a very serious error in judgment.

Some marry persons with whom they have had affairs. On the surface an affair can be psychologically, intellectually, and sexually fulfilling for persons with marital problems. It may fill specifically felt needs. It flourishes for a while. But the popular myth that an affair improves your marriage contains more fiction than fact.

Some marriages that stem from affairs can and do work; however, by and large, they are few. These relationships hold a high risk because of their foundation in motivations stemming from problems in the former marriage. Such relationships, based upon deception, eventually will be found out, causing pain and guilt. Marriage from an affair can never totally fulfill its potential, because the honesty and respect just is not there.

Before marrying one with whom you have had an affair, ask yourself:

1. How will your family—especially your children—accept the new person?
2. Do you really have enough in common to make a success in marriage?
3. Do you basically respect the other, in spite of the infidelity?
4. Can both be trusted not to have another affair once you marry? What will prevent it?

Equal preparation is necessary for marrying again as for an initial venture. If you do decide to marry again, may your motives be pure, your love sincere, and your devotion unwavering.

Reflection Guide 4

1. Have you been together in enough common, everyday, pleasant and unpleasant experiences to really know each other's feelings, habits, and attitudes well?

2. Do you like to visit each other's homes? Do the opposite parents really like you? Do you truly like them? What is the opinion of your parents?

3. Are your economic, cultural, geographical, and racial backgrounds similar?

4. Have you common interests and recreations that you both enjoy for long periods of time?

5. Do you agree on basic social and political beliefs, personal ideals, and views regarding life?

6. Have you dated many friends of the opposite sex, so you can compare and judge how you feel about each other in contrast to others?

7. Are you mature enough to undertake the responsibilities of marriage?

8. Is there more than ten years' difference in your ages? Is either under twenty years of age?

9. Is there anything about the personality of the other that bothers you? Have you tired of each other? Do you nag or criticize each other? Have you taken each other for granted?

10. Does the other possess all that you admire in a person? Have you made a wise choice?

4

Before Becoming Too Emotionally Involved

The old adage rings with a deep note of truth, "An ounce of prevention is worth a pound of cure." Choosing the right partner requires some basic studying and decision making before you become emotionally involved with just one person.

Use Your Head

A happy and enduring marriage begins with a good selection of a life mate. After you have "fallen in love," it is difficult to be sufficiently objective, reasonable, or logical. Of a truth, "Love is blind." Emotions run away with reason; the heart dominates the head. When you are in love, you'll have a tendency to overlook faults, to ignore danger signals that are obvious to others, and to dismiss the counsel of mature persons. Your rationalizations and self-justifications will warp the true assessment of yourself and your object of love.

Do It Early

If you are to use your head in making a wise mate selection, you need to do it early. The only time the intellect functions successfully is before, not after, you have become romantically entangled. The considerations and warnings delineated in this book and other marriage manuals should be digested before the more intimate, personal bonds develop; this way, many mistakes could be avoided. That kind of prevention starts long before a prospective mate ever appears.

Unconscious Development

Marriage decisions are seldom snap decisions. Your values and priority scales influence your decisions. The marriage of your parents, family friends, parents of peer groups, and the standards of peer groups all influence your choice of a life mate.

Actually your ideas about marriage began developing unconsciously, in childhood. They have been built into your whole system of life values by your parents, teachers, friends, companions, church, movies, TV, reading, and scores of other sources. The kind of adult friends your parents chose and the kind of playmates you were encouraged to play with constituted a process of selection. You chose as your friends the persons whom you liked and who liked you, because you had similar interests and cherished sharing time with each other.

In much the same way, you marry a person because you like her or him, not because you have gone around with a checklist in hand and have analyzed the qualifications. We marry persons, not abstractions. Even though you temper romance with common sense, this does not imply a cold, analytical approach.

You cannot let your mind totally rule emotions. One might, in cold, calculating fashion, select one of the opposite sex who perfectly fits the predetermined list of requirements. However, if the emotions are not drawn toward that person, the marriage probably would not succeed. Marriage selection is not like choosing an important employee or business partner. Essential in the selection is the force known as love, discussed in chapter six.

By the time a youth reaches marriageable age, his or her values are well established, and the type of person is fairly well determined, within some bounds. Nevertheless, give deliberate consideration to the whole matter of mate selection, to reenforce and reassure your life plan or to alter your decisions.

You cannot approach the selecting of a life mate as if blindly drawing from a gigantic grab bag, content that if you are unlucky the first time, you can come back and draw again. We want to eliminate that attitude.

Difficulties in Selecting a Mate

In ancient times the choice of a life mate was made by the parents. From a more mature perspective and with a breadth of acquaintances and experience, the parents chose marriage mates for their sons and daughters, sometimes before the youths ever met. In colonial America, the Puritan settlers did likewise for their children, a custom that regretfully still prevails in some areas of the world.

Parents should not determine the choice of spouses for their children. Parents can provide nondirective counsel when asked by a child, listening, helping objectify the factors, discussing important considerations, lifting up personality elements to contemplate. From the vantage point of experience, parents may deliberately suggest caution if they see obvious problems overlooked by their child. Parents must not aggressively give advice, nor should they be too opinionated; it is risky and may provoke ill will and resentment. In spite of all a parent may say in advance, the choice of a spouse ultimately lies with the individual contemplating marriage. But youths should seek the counsel of their parents, who should have the wisdom of years.

Freedom of Choice

Youths face a difficult problem in making such an important decision while still immature; being so, they may make immature choices. Maturity is marked by:

A capacity to look at one's self and one's problems objectively;

An ability to acknowledge and to control emotions;

An understanding of other people's feelings and a sensitive ability to respond to these emotions;

A growing independence from the control of family or friends;

A willingness to postpone immediate gratification so that a greater satisfaction can be attained in the future;

A responsible attitude toward sex;

A realistic and essentially positive self-image and an ability to make choices and live with the consequences of one's decisions.[7]

Some marriages go on the rocks not because the aggrieved partner did not get what he or she wanted; rather he did get what he wanted, but at the time of the choice he wanted the wrong things. The most significant factor in the actual choice of a mate is what you are. But one partner may, with maturity and increased responsibility, begin to cherish more serious values, while the other partner does not.

The best protection against unsound marriage is a serious, critical self-look to establish in yourself the values, attitudes, hopes, and characteristics required for responsible adult life. As Dr. Charlie Shedd says, "Marriage is not so much *finding* the right person as it is *being* the right person!"[8]

To have the responsibility of making one of life's most important decisions at any time, especially while young, is an awesome task, which should be approached prayerfully and with trusted counsel.

The mobility of our population makes the choice even more difficult today. This creates widely divergent values, unfamiliarity with family backgrounds, a temporary mentality, and a pluralism in many basic ingredients necessary to permanent marriage relationships. Ideas and ideals and degree of compatibility are really difficult to assess in such circumstances.

Sensuality

The sensuality dominating television, the movie screen, and publications, coupled with the increasing priorities of "free sex" and live-in arrangements easily obscure from the mind some essential considerations for a happy marriage. The extraordinary exploitation of sex appeal in our society frequently makes sex the only consideration. Physical attractiveness, popularity, and social status too often appear paramount, minimizing emotional stability, character, and disposition.

Sex attraction is important! Sex in reality forms the basis of all mating patterns. It is legitimate. Most marriages would never take place without it. Most couples marry because they find each other so attractive that they want to live together. Physical appeal is perhaps the most common lure to the initial contact and probably the chief factor in following up the relationship. Nevertheless, exploration of personality, backgrounds, convictions, emotions, and other facets need equal consideration.

Predictability

Clinical psychologists use scores of psychological and personality tests. Great strides have been made in the field of testing. The most common premarital tests used by church pastors include: "The Taylor-Johnson Temperament Test"; "The Myers-Briggs Marriage Expectation Inventory, Form I"; Gelolo McHugh, "Sex Knowledge Inventory"; "A Sex Attitude Survey and Profile"; and "The Pre-Marital Scoring Device." Yet all are far from being totally reliable. Exceptions to the rules always exist and experiences sometimes prove the warnings ill grounded. No list of desirable attributes fits every couple.

Guideposts

Nevertheless, the observations of experience constitute significant guideposts to point directions and provide helpful counsel. Though not always accurate, a pretty good assessment of the happiness of a marriage can be made in advance.

I have known from the very beginning that some marriages would end in divorce. It is obvious in advance. Not all people who want to marry are ready for marriage.

Major Considerations

LENGTH OF ACQUAINTANCE   Whirlwind courtships do not have a good record of success. The knowledge needed before engagement is not acquired in a hurry. A direct correlation between length of acquaintance before marriage and the success of marriage does exist. The proportion of well-adjusted marriages rises steadily with the increased period of acquaintance.

All of us have read in novels or seen in movies or observed in real life the short-term exposure: a couple meets, falls madly in love, and marries shortly thereafter. Typical is the TV's "Love Boat" episodes, where on an ocean voyage, two passengers are drawn to each other. A calm sea, a full moon, an absence of responsibility, and a sense of apartness from the world cause folk of all ages to be thrown together. Day after day, through varied recreation, activities, dancing, dining, and opportunities to talk, they pair off. In this temporary, unreal world, surrounded by seemingly unlimited distances, Cupid casts away all caution, and new romances result. As the TV portrayal reveals, engagements of months' standing are broken for new ones formed within days. Marriage partners are tempted to forsake their spouses for new loves. This thrilling but dangerous adventure supersedes most of the normal activities of life, does not allow for verification of cultural backgrounds, and requires that all be accepted or rejected on faith.

Prospective partners need to know each other in many ways and through many years.

FAMILY BACKGROUND   Each needs to know the other members of the family, most especially the parents. One marries the entire clan, like it or not. A congenial relationship and acceptance by in-laws is exceedingly important. In our mobile society this often becomes difficult to accomplish. One occasionally meets a couple planning to marry who has never met with the prospective in-laws, let alone developed a relationship. Under no circumstance should one become serious about marriage without taking time to know the family background and members.

DISPOSITION Each needs to know what the other might do under emotional strain. On dates couples see each other with their "best feet forward," but what is the other's disposition when things go wrong, when he or she faces thwarted desires, or if feelings are injured? Will she "freeze up" for a long period, or will she go into a rage and "blow her top?" Will he admit a mistake and easily soften into love and reconciliation? Will he resort to profanity, an "outburst of temper," to drink, or to illness? When faced with an ordeal, some people retreat into a world of fantasy.

GENERAL VIEWS Prospective partners need to know how they feel about politics, religious faith, the role of women, the role of husbands, the goals of life, each other's attitudes regarding sex, children, discipline, the accumulation of possessions, money, the church, and involvement in the community.

Don't be in a hurry. Take time to know each other, to see each other in all kinds of circumstances—good and bad. Said a sobbing bride who experienced the abusive outburst of her husband's temper, "I didn't know he was like that. It never showed up before we married."

Similarities

Dr. Tim LaHaye's book *Understanding the Male Temperament* describes the theory that there are four basic, opposing temperaments. He insists that opposites attract in marriage, and introverts often marry extroverts. As a marriage counselor, his research appears convincing in this area, which confirms Schopenhauer's theory.

Perhaps, when the opposite temperament characteristics are sufficiently tempered so that a meshing and adjusting of personalities is possible, this becomes feasible. However, research does not bear out the concept that because opposites interest each other and the characteristics of one complement those of the other they will therefore make the happiest couple. It is an interesting theory, but a poor fact. Individual variations within fairly narrow limits cause a definite attraction and may eliminate the dullness of complete uniformity, but the basic factors underlying harmonious union include common backgrounds and social values. Varied interests, when not too divergent, add spice to companionship, but a broad base of mutual interests and a common philosophy of life cement the union.

AGE   Concerning this subject, blanket assertions rarely prove helpful. The existence of certain successful marriages between partners of widely divergent ages cannot insure an exceptional degree of marital happiness for everyone in this situation. In fact, most individuals do not desire this kind of union. Frequently interests and activities present problems when ages are far apart. The man twenty years' his bride's senior may keep up with her initially, but when he is sixty and she is forty, difficulties may occur. Since women generally outlive men, a younger woman may face more years of widowhood. Perhaps a couple with more than ten years' difference in their ages should reconsider their decision to marry.

According to many studies, maximum happiness most often occurs in marriages where the husband is three to five years older than his spouse, though wives one to three years older than their husbands fail to prove marriage liabilities. Ideal ages for marriage vary, depending on the researchers, from twenty-five for the man and twenty-two for the woman, to twenty-nine for the man and twenty-four for the woman.

High rates of annulment, desertion, and divorce indicate marriage between two very young people tends to be unstable. Likewise, once the parties reach thirty-five, chances for divorce increase, because both are more set in their ways and find adjustments more difficult.

RACE AND NATIONALITY   Though love recognizes no lines of color or culture, it finds many practical difficulties in crossing racial and nationality boundaries. No biological ill effects result from interracial marriages, and they are now legal throughout the United States. This situation involves no moral question of right or wrong.

Even so, society being what it is and common family backgrounds being so profoundly important, those who marry outside their race set sail on a sea of trouble. They should scan the waters, clear eyed and realistically, before setting sail, realizing they face more unknown and potentially hazardous rocks than in the normal sea of matrimony. The couple must enjoy economic and social contacts and be an accepted part of the social fabric if they expect to live normally. The frictions, misunderstandings, and assumptions that seem so trivial, seen from a distance, loom large and forbidding when reached. The lack of continuity of cultural and family traditions frequently brings disaster. The children of interracial marriages are particularly handicapped. Interfamily strife and alienation increase within interracial marriages.

Great strides are being made in this country for acceptance of all kinds of racial combinations. Nonetheless, the similarity of race and national background gives greater promise of enduring happiness.

A Voluntary Choice

"There is one person in the world meant for you!" This outmoded theory set forth the concept that somewhere the person of your dreams waited just for you. It implied that if a young man wandered widely enough, he crossed the pathway of the waiting girl. Furthermore, they recognized each other at first sight and fell in love instantaneously. It just does not happen that way. Instead of being just one person in the world for you, probably several thousand persons of the same general culture and characteristics exist, whom you could admire and love; any one of them might make you happy if met and courted under favorable conditions. You have the responsibility to choose wisely. And remember, the choice is voluntary!

Freedom is the condition of love. A man may resent a woman who throws herself at him because she spoils, by her aggressiveness, his right to choose. A woman may instinctively hate a man who forces her into that which should occur with her own consent.

Reflection Guide 5

1. Do you agree on basic views regarding life? Do you have similar philosophic and ethical standards?
2. Do you understand, like, and appreciate each other's religious convictions?
3. Do you feel your love for each other has brought you closer to God?
4. What are the important religious values to marriage?
5. Do you bring out the best in each other?
6. Do you find joy in sharing common social, recreational, and religious interests?
7. Do you like to attend church together and be involved in service activities?
8. Will the church be an active part in the lives of both?
9. What are your main goals in life?
10. Do you believe you can best fulfill your God-given purpose in life married to this person?

5

The Spiritual Dimensions in Marriage

No single factor gives more stability to a married relationship than spiritual togetherness. The Apostle Paul admonished that married couples should not "... be mismated with unbelievers ..." (2 Corinthians 6:14). That means that if the husband and wife have faith in God, love the person of Jesus of Nazareth, are committed to Christian values, and share a common purpose in life, they have an essential foundation and far greater prospects for an enduring marriage. If one believes in God and the other does not, if one is committed to Christian morality and the other is not, if one is involved in the church and the other is not, then a couple will begin to live parallel lives. They will become separated in the very areas that provide the underlying unity, cementing their relationship together.

Being Equally Yoked

Belief in God as Creator and Father gives a vertical dimension to existence and a transcendent Being to whom each owes responsibility. To be a disciple of Jesus is to have commitment to personal integrity, reverence for personality, tolerance of human differences, tender compassion, unselfishness, and forgiveness. To have a sense of "at home-ness" in the universe and of being loved by God is to have self-esteem and a heart conditioned for loving and trusting. The filling of God's Holy Spirit gives each the ability to consistently demonstrate "... love, joy, peace, patience, kindness, goodness, faithfulness, gentleness, self-control." (Galatians 5:22, 23).

When couples realize that they have a God-given mission here on earth and are "co-workers together with God," it saves marriage from the mundaneness of purely "secular" living. Religiously oriented couples do not focus primarily on their own selfish, sensual pleasures. They share a thrill of adventure; life becomes a great stewardship of giving of themselves.

Dr. Howard Clinebell and his wife, Charlotte, assert that the Christian religion fills three basic needs in a marriage:

1. The need for an experience of transcendence.
2. The need for a sense of meaning, purpose, and values in one's existence.
3. The need for a feeling of deep trust and relatedness to life.[9]

From observation, we see that these spiritual commitments provide the warp and woof of the fabric of marriage. Let God be neglected, and the spiritual life becomes inoperable in marriage; as a result, that which binds husband and wife together will be quite tenuous and may crumble at the slightest provocation.

Spirit and Sex

The late Bishop Fulton Sheen once wrote a book entitled, *Three to Get Married,* in which he affirmed the spiritual dimension in sex. He said: "The attraction of a beast for a beast is physiological; the attraction of human to human is physiological, psychological and spiritual."[10] Love is primarily in the will, not in the emotions or the glands. The greatest illusion of lovers, Bishop Sheen asserts, is to believe that the intensity of their sexual attraction guarantees their enduring love. Because of this failure to distinguish between the glandular and spiritual—or between sex, which we have in common with animals, and love, which we have in common with God—marriages sometimes become tenuous.

As soon as the glands cease to react with exciting force, couples who identify emotionalism as love claim they no longer love each other. "If such is the case, they never truly loved the other person in the first place; they only loved being loved. Marriage based only on sex passion alone, lasts only as long as the fleshly passions last."[11] When the physical attraction for the other dwindles and there is no spiritual dimension to the relationship, divorce usually results. "Those who separate the spiritual from sex are rehearsing death."[12]

God Is Love

No human being on earth today entirely personifies love. Humans may be lovable, but only God is Love.

When we put the creature in the place that only the Creator can occupy, we experience disillusionment. When one's partner is discovered to be a woman instead of an angel or to be a man with feet of clay instead of Apollo, a desire for a new partner begins. When the ecstasy loses its glamor and the champagne of life loses its sparkle, the assumption surfaces that some other human being can supply what only God can give.

Not in the changing of partners will we find love. The source of love is God. We learn to love because He loves us. We become lovable because we experience being loved by God.

Two empty glasses cannot fill each other. There must be a fountain outside the glasses to supply and to continually renew love. That is why "it takes three to make love."

Involvement Together

Religious values operating in each of the partners show great value in marriage, as does the couple's involvement in the same church. Experience reveals some discernible factors concerning joint religious allegiance:

1. A couple who worships God together experience the Source of love, which is the basic support of a marriage relationship.
2. The services of the church communicate much on both the unconscious and conscious levels, which nourishes in a couple sound personal attitudes and values that bear directly upon a good marriage. Both partners need similar exposure.
3. A tie-in with a group of Christian people committed to the same ethical views and influenced by the same motivations supports the marriage relationship.
4. Participation in the church's ministry of compassion and service creates a wholesome unselfishness for spouses.

Hence, belonging to the same denominational church minimizes destructive influences and maximizes stabilizing values.

Reflection Guide 6

1. Do you recognize the difference between infatuation and love?

2. Is yours a deep and abiding love for the whole person?

3. When you are separated, do you long to be with the other?

4. Are you constantly wanting to make the other happy and to buy love tokens, even after a reasonably long going steady period?

5. When separated for a few weeks or months, does your interest lessen? Do you date or want to date others during this time?

6. During separation, are your thoughts completely absorbed in the other? Are you faithful in correspondence or calls?

7. Can you project compatible companionship and faithful devotion with the other over thirty or fifty years, even when looks and vitality have changed?

8. Are you spontaneously affectionate and thoroughly companionable?

9. Are you always proud to introduce each other to your family, friends, and church members? Do you respect each other's cultural or professional attainments? Is there any jealousy of each other?

10. What does "I love you" mean to you?

6

Are You in Love?

Dear Abby,

We just celebrated our 10th wedding anniversary, and I'm terribly depressed. I was 20 and J was 33 when he swept me off my feet. He proposed on our third date with a 5-carat diamond ring in his pocket. I was stunned and asked for a week to think it over. I knew I didn't love him and told my mother so. She said I would learn to love. She was wrong.

J was (and still is) crazy about me. I have a beautiful home and more clothes, furs and jewelry than I can wear.

J is a very homely man. He's short (I never wear heels), overweight, bald and wears very thick glasses. (Contacts don't work for him.) He is kind, considerate and faithful, and he tells me he loves me every day. He owns a business that paid him a $175,000 salary last year, and he's generous beyond belief. He's been wonderful to my family too.

I admire J, respect him and appreciate him. But I don't *love* him. Sometimes I dream of leaving him, but I could never do it. We have two beautiful children I could never give up. Besides, it would be unfair to take them from their father.

I feel terribly guilty—as though I'm playing a part. I want to see a psychiatrist, but J would ask me what was troubling me and I could never tell him. Please help me.

DEPRESSED.[13]

Love or Illusion?

Are you in love, or is it an illusion? When you exchange the sentiment "I love you," what do you really mean? What are the elements of love?

Love is an abstract quality. Mention *love* in contemporary society, and each person gives a different definition. It almost defies description. Some associate it totally with sex and romance. Some name it a sentimental feeling for someone. Some use the word in conjunction with material objects, such as "I love music, books, and animals."

The ancient Greeks had three words to sharpen their ideas of love. *Phileo* described a parent's love for a child or a child's for his parents or a child's for a child. From this we get our word *filial. Eros* was used to depict the love between sweethearts or a husband and wife. It had to do with romantic feelings. From it we get our word *erotic.* Then the word *agape* characterized compassionate caring for others, regardless of the quality of their lives or their likableness. It describes Christian goodwill and God's love for humanity.

In English we use the word *love* for all these facets of the human spirit.

Too often, perhaps, we assume that a warm, romantic feeling is tantamount to love. People say they have fallen in love, when maybe they have only "fallen into lust." Physical attractiveness exerts such a power that someone handsome or beautiful taking an interest in us may sweep us off our feet.

"It was love at first sight," we say. There is no such thing. "I knew I had to have her as my wife when I first laid eyes upon her." That person has merely fallen in love with love. "I can't explain it," she said, "but we just have the right body chemistry for each other." None of these descriptions, based more on illusion than love, more on emotion than reason, adequately portray a love sufficient to guarantee an enduring or happy marriage.

Love is a mystical attraction comprised of physical, mental, social and spiritual elements. Love consists of respect for and devotion to the total person. It is emotion, but not emotion devoid of reason.

Distinguishing Between Love and Infatuation

A physical, sexual attraction usually begins relationships. A fellow is attracted to a girl initially by her looks and trim figure. The handsomeness or athletic physique of a boy captures a girl's attention. They easily confuse this infatuation with love. Much of what is called love is nothing more than a confused mixture of sentimental pathos, disguised egotism, Freudian complexes, and weakness of character.

Infatuation focuses primarily on physical attraction and blinds itself to many other factors that should be considered for marriage. Accompanied by an emotional crush more adolescent than mature, more romantic than responsible, more subjective than objective, infatuation thinks in terms of immediacy and often stampedes the other with passionate demands. Usually short-lived and fickle, the thrill wears off quickly.

The infatuated couple tends to isolate themselves from others. They become indifferent and even hostile to the advice of parents and friends. Often these persons insist upon a hasty marriage and threaten elopement if their demands are delayed. With infatuation, emotion controls; reason goes out the window.

When a boy or girl makes sexual demands, that very fact usually indicates sexual infatuation, which makes marriage prospects very tenuous. Sometimes this kind of infatuation deepens into love that has other dimensions, but do not bank on it.

True Love

True love, on the other hand, considers what is best from the long-term perspective, listens, maintains flexibility with plans, and controls sex impulse for mutual benefit.

What are the signs of true love? A few of them follow:

You feel a mental, social, and spiritual attraction, as well as a physical attraction to the person.

You desire to be with each other constantly, always thinking of the other and wanting to make him or her happy.

You share many common interests, can converse about a broad base of similar experiences and beliefs, and enjoy some of the same recreations.

You may proudly introduce each other to people and want to date each other steadily; you yearn to know the family and clan of your prospective partner and take a genuine interest in the family history.

You are spontaneously affectionate.

You do not criticize each other or constantly argue; instead you bring out the best in each other and encourage each other.

You constantly buy love tokens, with true love, and want to take your loved one to special events.

With true love, you feel more alive, enthusiastic, interested in the future, and closer to the meaning of life.

Testing Your Love

Before making a firm decision regarding your choice of a life mate, apply the following tests:

THE TEST OF TIME   Real love grows over a long period of time. If during a reasonably long courtship, you still admire the qualities of thoughtfulness, unselfishness, generosity, and sincerity, you desire to do nothing to disappoint the other, and you seek every possible way to make the other happy—and if the other does the same—this indicates genuine love. Both must feel the same, or love is only one-sided.

THE TEST OF SEPARATION   Be separated for a few weeks or months to see whether your interest lessens. If your thoughts remain completely absorbed in the other, in spite of separation, if you both correspond or call faithfully, if you have no interest in seeing or dating anyone else during the interim, it is true love.

THE TEST OF COMPANIONSHIP If you feel the desire to be together constantly and can project this feeling over thirty to fifty years of companionship, even when looks and vitality have changed, this indicates true love.

A Religious Matter

Love should bring you closer to God. The very center of Christian faith is love—for God is love. Falling in love then ought to be a very religious experience.

We enjoy many other essentially religious experiences. God touches our consciousness when we are awed by a beautiful rose or a multicolored sunset or when we enjoy a glorious rendition of good music or look into the eyes of a little child. But God breaks through more powerfully in the love of another. Acceptance, a sense of worth, a feeling of being cherished express love.

Such love reveals itself in the physical as well as psychological, for both share a divine element. In one mood love may express itself as a tumultuous passion and in another a beautiful, calm, mysterious joy. Whatever it is, it is divine.

The wedding ceremony contains the phrase "love, honor, and cherish." A person cannot really and truly love another deeply and consistently unless he or she *honors,* meaning "to esteem, appreciate, and respect," the other and *cherishes,* meaning "to prize, hold dear, and nurture," the other.

Love and Sex Contrasted

Love ultimately includes sex, but sex does not always include love. Sex concentrates upon function, while love concentrates upon personality. Sex is subjective, directed to the self for self-gratification, while love is objective, directed to someone else for the sake of the other's satisfaction and perfection.

Sex receives so as not to give; love gives and in the process receives.

The desire to fill a moment between having and not having motivates sex. Having been filled by the experience, it rests for a moment and then waits for the reappearance of a new craving to be satisfied again—perhaps by a totally different partner. Pleasure drives sex.

Love is directed to the totality of the person—body, mind, and soul—and seeks mutual joy with an exclusive companion.

How sad the lot of persons who have sex without love, most pronounced in the woman who has been made a tool of pleasure alone, not a companion of love. She experiences humiliation in realizing that any other woman could fulfill her role; for sex without love lacks anything personal, communicable, dignified, or deeply meaningful. Every woman instinctively realizes the difference between love with sex and sex devoid of love.

Reflection Guide 7

1. Is the purpose of your engagement to confirm your choice of a potential life mate?
2. Is there anything about the personality of the other that might hinder a happy and enduring marriage? Can alcohol, gambling, or drugs become a potential problem?
3. Have you tired of the other during the engagement period? Does he or she get on your nerves?
4. Do you nag or criticize each other? Do you argue a lot?
5. Have you taken each other for granted? Do you still treat the other respectfully, tenderly, and unselfishly? and vice versa?
6. Is one of you reluctant to marry, and is the other pushing? Do you both really want to marry, or is it one-sided?
7. Is either of you looking toward marriage as an escape from a situation you do not like?
8. Are you thoroughly compatible? Are you willing to be with the other every day for the remainder of your life?
9. Are there any inner doubts? Would you "break it off" now, if you had the courage?
10. Are you proceeding on the assumption that, after marriage, you can change what you do not like in the other? that somehow things will work out?

7

Confirming Your Choice

Choosing the person and developing a relationship that will last is a process.

In this age of immediacy—with instant coffee, instant banking, fast food—some would like a short-term courtship and instant response to the question "Will you marry me?" It just does not happen that way; and if it does, it signifies a risky venture.

Lana Turner, a sex symbol of Hollywood a generation ago, married seven times. Her first marriage was to band leader Artie Shaw, on their first date. She said in a recent "Today Show" interview that she didn't like him, much less love him and that she knew on the third day it was not a marriage. It lasted three months. In retrospect she admits that she was a "fool" for marrying hurriedly and for unworthy motives—security, handsomeness, and glamor. She did not take the time to develop her relationships before her seven marriages. Had she done so, the incompatibilities and weaknesses would have come to light. Her interview closed with this statement, "When respect is gone, love goes out the door."

Have You Played the Field?

Some people marry the only person they ever dated. As a general rule this is unwise. You should date and get to know a number of different people before narrowing the field. Spend several years dating, because your ideas will mature and change. Playing the field gives you an opportunity to contrast different personalities, assess values, determine likes and dislikes, and to experience the different emotional responses you have to a variety of persons. While dating many people, you grow in the art of conversation and conviction; your personality develops. Each person is different, and you relate to some better than others. Some bring out your best, some your worst. As you date, your emotional repertoire develops. Under these circumstances, you can more intelligently choose the potentially best marriage partner.

Another mistake that men and women often make is to view every new person as a potential marriage partner. On this basis, if the person does not look right or strike an instant romantic attraction, he or she is cut off immediately, with no chance given for developing a relationship. You may overlook the very qualities that would make for a congenial mate; these can be discerned only by dating. Having marriage constantly on the mind can become a deterrent to the kind of relaxed friendship and exploration necessary for getting to know each other well.

Testing Compatibility

Once you limit your dating to one person, you start to develop an emotional attachment. You begin what used to be called "going steady," because you mutually prefer each other to others. You put yourself out of circulation from dating others.

Some people go steady so they can be sure of a date. Others find it cheaper and easier than dating a variety of persons. Others gain a psychological security in the ability to attract one of the opposite sex. Still others do so to live up to group or family expectations.

Narrowing the field to one steady date can test compatibility. Each explores more in depth the other's sense of humor, tastes, values, backgrounds, ambitions, fears, and hopes without intrusion of competition. It is for having a good time. As interest in each other deepens, you gain the understanding that precedes engagement. Thus going steady facilitates the selection of a promising marriage mate.

Breaking Up

Dating people not uncommonly fall in and out of "going steady" many times. It may be advisable or necessary before making your final choice.

In breaking off a serious relationship, you face an extremely traumatic experience, especially after an emotional dependence has evolved. Sometimes a domineering, inflamed person threatens the hesitant partner. The pain of confrontation precipitates some into going ahead with an obviously unequally yoked marriage, doomed from the outset. But the discomfort of a split at this stage is infinitely preferable to a broken engagement or divorce.

If you entertain serious doubts, have no complete inner concurrence, or are involved in a one-sided relationship, muster the courage to break off, however many the tears. If your interests and love are not reciprocal, you have slim chances for a happy marriage.

On the verge of marriage, you experience strong hunches, either positive or negative. Intuitively this step seems right and you experience peace about it, or you feel a deep-seated hesitation. Your unconscious signals your conscious in this way. Pay attention to negative signals; they are red flags warning you to caution or a halt.

Engagement With Purpose

If through the going-steady period, you have found mutual understanding and a broad base of common interests and are in love, you may declare your intentions to marry with engagement. The intention is formalized and made known publicly.

The engagement period has several recognized purposes,

important as preludes for a harmonious marriage. First it presents you as a pair in the eyes of family and friends. You seriously look ahead to marriage and develop a *we* feeling as you make plans together.

Further acquaintance with each other's history, clan, true circumstances, and basic philosophies becomes possible. Sharing of good times and troubles, dreams and disappointments, ambitions and failures allows a firsthand participation in the other's character. You learn to talk freely and work together for common interests, weaving a bond of companionship.

Giving and receiving affection is a vital part of engagement. You should approach marriage ready for the full intimacy of marriage, physically and emotionally.

Engagement involves planning for the wedding, plus discussing all the relevant questions regarding budget, housing, employment, birth control, children, church, in-laws, and so on. The planning before marriage establishes the patterns you carry over into your permanent relationship.

The engagement period should confirm or deny your decision about marriage. Many clues emerge, during engagement, concerning the likelihood of success or failure.

If at this stage your heart does not completely concur with your actions, do not ignore it. Not until the areas of doubt are cleared up and complete confidence is restored should you proceed to the altar. Better to break a heart by breaking an engagement than to break a life (or two or three or more) by breaking a marriage.

Premarital Counseling

In my judgment premarital counseling is imperative, preferably long before any wedding plans are made. Several sessions should take place during a couple's early serious courtship, not later than the early engagement months, before definite dates are set.

Counseling may assess compatibility and inspire frank and open conversations about sharing life together. Couples, of course, should read much about marriage (*see* Recommended Reading at the end of this book). Beyond the reading is the necessity for talking out and vocalizing the areas covered, in the presence of an experienced, trusted counselor, preferably with the minister who will perform the marriage ceremony.

Considerations may surface in the counseling process that will alter viewpoints, reveal areas of weakness, or give cause for caution. It thus gives time for making needed adjustments. It may cause an indefinite delay. Remember, it is better to discover the problems before they arrive.

Premarital Scoring Device[14]

1. How many brothers and sisters do you have?

	NONE	ONE	TWO OR MORE
MAN	0	10	15
WOMAN	0	10	15

2. Comparative national and cultural backgrounds

	SAME	FAIRLY SIMILAR	VERY DISSIMILAR
BOTH	20	10	0

3. Comparative amount of education

BOTH THE SAME	MAN MORE THAN WOMAN	WOMAN MORE
15	10	0

4. Comparative ages

SIMILAR	VERY DISSIMILAR
15	5

5. Comparative occupations

BOTH SAME TYPE	FAIRLY SIMILAR	VERY DISSIMILAR
10	5	0

6. Work record

	REGULARLY EMPLOYED	IRREGULARLY EMPLOYED
MAN	(20)	0
WOMAN	(10)	5

7. How long have you known each other? (Based on frequent associations.)

6 MOS. OR LESS	6 MOS.– 1 YR.	1–3 YRS.	3 YRS. OR MORE
(0)	(5)	10	20

8. How long have you been engaged?

1–3 MOS.	3 MOS.– 1 YR.	1–2 YRS.	2 YRS. OR MORE
(0)	15	10	5

9. Number of social organizations to which both belong

NONE	ONE	TWO OR MORE
0	(10)	15

10. Present amount of religious activity

	MAN	WOMAN
NOT A MEMBER, AND NO ATTENDANCE	0	0
MEMBER, BUT NO ATTENDANCE AT CHURCH	5	5
ATTEND NO MORE THAN ONCE A MONTH	10	10
ATTEND TWO OR MORE TIMES A MONTH	25	20
ATTEND FOUR OR MORE TIMES A MONTH	(30)	(25)

11. Will you both attend the same church?

YES	NO, BUT BOTH PROTESTANT	ONE CATHOLIC
(50)	25	0

12. Is either person a nonbeliever?

YES	NO
0	(50)

13. Until what age did you regularly attend Sunday school?

	10 or Under	14 or Under	19 or Under
Man	0	10	(20)
Woman	0	(10)	20

14. How would you rate your parents' marriage?

	Happy	Average	Unhappy	Divorced
Man	20	10	5	(0)
Woman	20	(10)	5	0

15. Do your parents favor your proposed marriage?

	Yes	No
Man	(10)	5
Woman	(15)	0

16. How do you get along with each other's parents?

	Very Well	Not So Well	Unacquainted	Dislike Them
Man	20	10	(5)	0
Woman	20	10	(5)	0

17. Do you double-date with other couples?

Often	Occasionally	Never
10	(5)	0

18. What hobbies do you have in common?

None	One	Two	Three or More
0	5	(10)	(15)

19. How have you handled disagreements during your courtship?

Have Had None	One Gives In	Talk It Through
(0)	5	(15)

20. Does the wife plan to work outside the home after marriage?

    Yes   No
    0   5

21. Who will be in charge of finances in your home?

    Husband   Wife   Cooperatively
    0   0   10

22. How many children do you hope to have?

    1   2   3 or More   None
    5   10   15   0

23. Will you live with either of your parents during the first year or so?

    Yes   No
    0   20

24. What books have you read on the subject of physical adjustment in marriage?

    None   1 or 2
    0   10

25. Has either person been married before?

    Yes   No
    0   25

26. Why did you come to a pastor to be married?

    Custom   Parents Did   Desire God's Blessing
    0   0   10

27. Do you plan to say grace at meals and have family devotions?

    Both   Neither   Grace
    20   0   10

28. Do you ever use prayer to help solve your problems?

	FREQUENTLY	OCCASIONALLY	NEVER
MAN	20	10	0
WOMAN	20	10	0

29. Would you like to have the pastor who marries you call on you in your home?

YES	NO
5	0

This guide is published by Fortress Press, 2900 Queen Lane, Philadelphia, Pa. 19129. The highest possible total scores on all twenty-nine questions are: Man 155, Woman 145, Both 370. Adding these three scores together we arrive at a total of 670. Most well-matched couples get a score of about 550. The purpose of the guide is to help the minister get to know the couple better, to encourage the couple to express themselves, to insure coverage of all important subjects and to eliminate the lecture form of counseling. Each minister may use the guide in a different way. Most rephrase the questions. Some give copies of the guide to the couples.

Low scores do not necessarily mean future unhappiness. The guide will serve to alert the couple to some possible points of friction which can be overcome by mature love and Christian understanding. If the score is frightfully low, the minister may be able to convince the couple that they are not quite ready and ought to wait six months or so.

HIGHEST POSSIBLE SCORE	670
EXCELLENT SCORE	above 575
GOOD SCORE	425 to 575
FAIR SCORE	325 to 425
QUESTIONABLE SCORE	below 325

520 →

Reflection Guide 8

1. . Does either person have a reputation for being contentious or a troublemaker?
2. Do both get along well with the other's family and friends?
3. Are you unselfish, willing to give and take and compromise for the sake of peace? Is your partner likewise?
4. Can you talk about differences in a calm, objective way?
5. What will you do after you have an argument?
6. Can you adjust your differences promptly, without bitterness or lingering anger and resentment?
7. How skilled are you in conflict management?
8. Are you able to admit wrong and to say, "I am sorry"?
9. Do you find it easy to forgive one who has wronged you?
10. Have you developed a real *we* consciousness?

8

Constructive Problem Solving

A famous judge once said, "Every couple is sometime on the way to the divorce court. However, it is the big-spirited people who learn to face their problems constructively and to transcend their differences."

Occasionally one hears an old-timer boast, "We've never had an argument in all our years of marriage." One can only conclude that such a person has a poor memory, has completely dominated the relationship, is lying, or has an unbearably boring marriage.

Even if your fiancé is in most respects ideal for you, with few basic incompatibilities, problems will still occur. Strong differences take place between husband and wife, even occasionally among the most sanctified. It is only human. Two personalities do not blend easily, nor is it expected or desirable that they should be exact duplicates in their thoughts, feelings, or habits.

The difference between an unsuccessful and a successful marriage is not that the former includes serious problems and the latter lacks them. Rather, successfully married couples develop skills in handling problems. Virtually all problems are potentially solvable, if a couple devotes enough time and energy to examining the causes and working on them.

Conflicts Inevitable

Conflict in marriage is inevitable, for no two persons want exactly the same things or see the world exactly the same way. Constructively used conflict should form a means of communication and deepening of the bonds of intimacy. Anger in marriage may expose the truth and open communications so that a problem can be healed. Silent, smoldering resentments often destroy emotional health and a relationship.

Some assume they know their partners "like a book," so ignore the unresolved differences. But the task of exposing, then conquering, the conflict needs to be honestly faced.

Conflict can be destructive or constructive. Before you open up and reveal anger, consider whether discussion will improve or hinder the relationship. Some mates attack their partners because they want to diminish and hurt them. They engage in name calling, ridicule, and belittling, cruel practices, not to improve the relationship, but rather to triumph over the other and to seek vengeance.

When one person has a gripe or when an argument is brewing, the questions to ask are: "Is this really something worth arguing about? Must this irritation be solved? Am I being petty or vengeful? Is this a fault in my partner or in me? Is solving this problem worth the price? Will the solution improve our relations with each other?"[15]

Lots of differences cannot be changed. Some can be overcome by mutual adjustments, growth, and understanding. There is no point in arguing about them. "Couples who value their relationship more than their differences will not engage in 'dirty fighting.' "[16] Highly sensitive points should not be deliberately exploited by an angry mate. Hitting below the belt will only hurt rather than improve the relationship. Some subjects should be "off limits" to discuss, for harmony's sake. The book of Ecclesiastes says there is ". . . a time to keep silence, and a time to speak" (3:7). Those who value their marriages will learn how to handle their anger in a fruitful way.

We *Consciousness*

When married, it is no longer *I,* but *we.* Marriage begins a new partnership. Perhaps, as a single individual, you have had only yourself to consider. You have had your own money, your own automobile, your own living expenses, your own budget, your own schedule, your own food tastes, your own clothing, your own insurance. You have been a self-centered individual.

Now you face marriage, and all that will change. You will be in union with another. A *we* consciousness must develop, because now you have to consider mutual tastes, two schedules, double expenses. You have to expand your sympathies, considerations, and hopes to include the welfare of two persons. This requires a shift in priorities, a recentering of life, a subordination, many times, of your own wishes. Before purchases are made or decisions concluded or plans projected, the other's wishes must be considered. Generosity and democracy become imperative practices. The enduring marriage requires a large measure of give-and-take. In marriage unselfishness is the indispensable ingredient.

Developing Problem-Solving Skills

Self-Control

The most important assets in solving marriage problems are the abilities to control emotions, to not overreact, and to be objective. Marital disturbances often result from problems with outside people or events and the manner in which persons react to them. Sometimes everyone needs an opportunity to give vent to pent-up feelings, by blowing up, crying, throwing a temper tantrum, or just talking to get it all out of one's system. You need to let go, even in expressing dissatisfaction, so your mate knows what you are thinking. Do not hold it all within yourself.

But objectivity cannot reign in the midst of emotion. When

overpowering feelings control you, let them subside before approaching a discussion. Self-control must prevail if you wish to avoid irrational behavior and wish to achieve solutions. Practice talking over some smaller, less emotion-charged issues first; then you may move on to issues involving deeper resentments.

The angry outburst, the thoughtless, cutting remark, the seemingly unprovoked attack, the sharp retort—all issue forth from us at times, no matter our level of love or commitment. These are symptoms of our sinful nature. Words wound—even unintentional ones—and once released, one cannot recall them or wipe them out.

Focusing on the Issue

Couples often allow pride to get in the way. Each becomes threatened, hence self-defensive and irrational, leading to violent quarreling. They never address the basic issue.

Learn to stay on the subject, instead of generalizing your complaints into sweeping accusations. Your partner, placed on the defensive, may launch into a counterattack that has nothing to do with the original issue. Thus the argument becomes personality centered. Minor incidents balloon into serious altercations. When you argue, make sure you fight over the actual issues involved.

Objectify the issues, apart from personalities, and focus on the problem in a calm, intelligent manner. It is easier said than done. Sorting out the basic issue may be difficult. The true roots causing the quarrel may be largely hidden. For this reason even exceptionally intelligent couples should have premarital counseling, to help each to get a clear understanding of the nature of their quarrels and to help them focus on the issues.

Open Communication

The most important of all skills in problem solving is effective communication between mates. An old adage says, "It takes two to make an argument." It also takes two to make a discussion, to work out a solution to a problem, and to negotiate a workable compromise. If one party to a marriage fails to communicate adequately, the relationship can grow brittle. When disturbances ruffle a marriage, silence is not necessarily golden. Just being willing to talk about the problem does not solve it, but it may help.

Each partner must recognize the existence of a difficulty about which communication is required. Often one mate tends to deny or to ignore a problem until it looms to threatening proportions. Some of us feel insecure and find it easier to hide our heads than to face the difficulty and talk it out. For many men, the relationship has to be terribly bad before they will seriously consider cooperating in communication.

Accusations or putting the other down will inflame the relationship. Two skills in communication are the willingness to assume most of the blame, even if it is not yours, and to assume the best in your partner. This disarming approach helps you refrain from saying what you do not truly mean to say, something for which you will be sorry. Quite easily one individual becomes threatening, making indefensible statements that must be supported. No one likes to backtrack; it is a blow to pride to do so, hence the human reacts with stubborn ego defensiveness.

Keeping positive about your mate, sandwiching your complaints in the midst of praise, and affirming the other's worth will get you far in constructive problem solving. An unscheduled telephone call, an unpredicted "happy gift," and small courtesies will help communicate worth to the other.

Respect for Individuality

For love and companionship to develop and flourish in marriage, intercommunication must root in respect for the individuality and personality of the spouse. Each mate must learn to proceed on the conviction that nothing warrants the violation of the mate's integrity. The *person* in each personality really matters. The individual's likes and dislikes, preferences and distastes, ideas and attitudes are unique and must be respectfully and lovingly honored.

Shared Humor

A good sense of humor can oil many troubled waters. If a couple has the capacity to withdraw from the situation and see how utterly ridiculous the quarreling is in the long perspective and if they can actually laugh at their behavior, it will do amazingly much to release tension. This does not mean that we become flippant about serious difficulties. Nor does it mean that it takes a third-rate comedian to succeed in modern marriage. It means that humor is one of the best methods of reducing anxiety blockage.

Sometimes couples need to take a less grim view of marriage and enjoy the relationship. They need to learn to humor each other. If one partner has had a bad day, the other should sense the mood and treat him or her with good humor. Be able to kid and tease a bit and assume the attitude "let's not be too grim about our problems." Share some laughs. Insert a funny story or happening. Laugh at yourself.

Forgiveness

When conflicts get out of control in marriage, the only way the storm can be stilled is for one partner to break the cycle of mutual attack. If it is ugly word for ugly word, retaliation for hurt rendered, the fight cannot be brought satisfactorily to an end.

When the storm breaks out, forgiveness must operate. The ability to accept a wound and to pardon and forget without seeking to retaliate is the essence of love.

Forgiveness in Christian marriage finds its model in the forgiveness God offers us in Christ Jesus. One offers forgiveness despite the pain and suffering borne, and blots the offenses of the mate from memory. The love of Christ in our hearts is its motivating power. Only forgiveness breaks the cycle of mutual attacks between mates; it brings with it repentance and the ability to say, "I'm sorry. I'll try not to do it again."

Reflection Guide 9

1. Do you enjoy job security? Will your income be adequate to meet your married needs?
2. Have you mutually decided how the family income will be budgeted? Have you plans for life insurance, health insurance, savings? What about support for your church, other charities, and for those dependent upon you? Will there be a household account?
3. Who will do the buying, paying of bills, keeping the records? Do you conceive of the household to be ruled by the husband, wife, or shared democratically?
4. Are you in sympathy with the occupation that the other has planned? Will both work? Will you work together in the care of home and children?
5. Will you arrange to live by yourselves and not with your parents? Where will that be?
6. Will you both join the same church? What church will it be? Do you have basic differences?
7. Do you plan to take an active part in the church?
8. What plans do you have for finding high-principled friends for the family you are about to establish?
9. Are you prepared to accept your in-laws as parents and to get along well?
10. What helpful adjustments can you make before you are married?

9

Adjustments Before Marriage

A couple must expect the need for adjustments in marriage. Many difficulties can be worked out, perhaps even before marriage.

Church Commitment

Astonishingly sometimes couples fall in love and talk about marriage without either one even knowing the other's church affiliation.

Research confirms that similarity in religious values is essential to a happy, divorce-proof marriage. Those who enter into mixed-faith marriages (Christian–Jewish, Christian–Moslem, Christian–Hindu, and so on) have far more chance of divorce than those who marry within their own faith. Likewise persons from widely divergent denominational churches (Roman Catholic–Baptist, Episcopal–Pentecostal, Methodist–Church of Christ) inevitably face religious difficulties. The risks escalate when one partner is Christian and the other has no religious commitments or church ties; this lends credence to the Apostle Paul's admonition, "Do not be mismated with unbelievers . . ." (2 Corinthians 6:14).

The adjustment to a common church membership is advisable before a couple marries. If not done before marriage, they can drift for years without any meaningful commitment. If one spouse, after marriage, suggests getting together in a church and developing the "church-going habit," it becomes nagging and potentially a subject of argument.

Especially when persons and their families are well grounded in their denominations and faiths, they may face a difficult choice. Only the couple is capable of making the decision. Their parents cannot make it, however good their intentions may be. A minister cannot make it, for he has a natural bias. A couple sufficiently mature to make a choice for marriage can make a church decision for their union's welfare.

If one or the other is more deeply committed and involved in his or her denomination and church, it might be advisable for the spouse to study that tradition and join with him or her. If both are involved and unable to give readily, it may be prudent to compromise on a neutral tradition that would not offend either and would respect the basic general convictions of both. If one party gives in to the other, perhaps one will conclude that the other has a superior denomination and unconscious resentment may brood.

Without compromise, if each retains his or her own direction, experience shows that religion becomes essentially inoperative in one or both parties' lives. When the children come along, they become confused about their parents' divided loyalties and begin taking sides.

The most important reason for getting together in the same faith and church is to share the same experiences, to be exposed to the same lessons, to participate together in worship, and to develop mutual friends so the family can grow and deepen in the basic meaning and purpose of life. You will have mutual friends of high ethical standards and service commitments, so the likelihood of romantic triangles developing lessens. Religious faith nurtures the cement that holds marriage together. Children grow up in a natural atmosphere of religious life.

Vocational Work

Will the wife work? Perhaps 80 percent of newly married women are part of the work force. Many young women are career oriented. Some resent the stereotyped role of home-maker. They want to combine a career with marriage and raising children. Sylvia Porter, the well-known economist, reports that more than 35 million women are employed. This is fine, if both husband and wife are prepared to make the adjustments.

The family life-style needs to be considered before marriage, so the implications are understood.

When both husband and wife have careers, the household responsibilities must be shared. It is quite unfair if the wife has to prepare the meals, do the cleaning, wash the laundry, and do the other multitudinous duties. The husband must carry 50 percent of the responsibility. What happens if his schedule does not coincide? What if one consistently gets home late? What about transportation to and from work?

Another factor to consider: What happens if one gets a promotion out of the city, to a faraway location, requiring a move? Whose career is to be primary? Will this become a problem? If so, how can you amicably resolve it? Will the husband or the wife feel resentment at the sacrifice of his or her work? Will resentment and remorse grow through the years if one career falters when the other might have taken him or her to the top?

Perhaps the most likely problem arising from both husband and wife working concerns finding time for sex when both are in the mood. When both feel weary from a long day's work and when neither is available during the day or when they merely pass each other going to and from work, it places tremendous strains (and often temptations) upon a marriage.

It takes time to improve sexual artistry for mutual enjoyment, a difficult feat in our frantic society. Setting aside time for regular "let's enjoy each other" nights or days will pay big dividends in a better marriage.

One couple, having experienced the difficulty, concluded

marriage counseling with the confession, "Up until we started having 'our nights,' sex got the tag end of our time. We allowed other, less important things to squeeze lovemaking into late, hurried moments, which made it terribly mechanical. In the last months we've discovered what we've been missing. Wow!"

Money

It has been said, "Two can live as cheaply as one, but only if one does not eat." Then comes the argument: "Which one does not eat?" Naive couples, oblivious to the costs of living, have said jokingly, "We will live on love."

One should not marry without profitable, secure employment and without projecting realistic expenses for beginning married life. Nothing strains a marriage like the pressure of creditors. The adjustment to a simpler standard of living is wrought with pain. The discipline of lessening material desires becomes weary even for those head over heels in love. Money may not compose all of married life, but life without it cannot long endure.

Prior to marriage, a couple should assess income, then determine a budget to give direction to the expenditures and to eliminate immature spending habits. A budget can never be, nor should it be, ironclad. It should have some flexibility and uncommitted residue for emergencies. Usually living as a couple will cost more than you project. Included in the budget, obviously, will be housing, food, transportation, clothing, insurance, maintenance, personal needs, recreation and entertainment, gifts, newspapers, magazines, books, church and charitable giving, taxes, plus savings and investments.

At the outset of marriage, a Christian couple should include giving to the church and other benevolent agencies. Giving a small amount at the beginning, perhaps a percentage of income, then increasing the percentage through the years, is wise.

Fewer people will be able to afford buying a home. Though it is the dream of every couple, no more than 30–35 percent of one's income should go toward home ownership. A few years ago financiers recommended not more than 20 percent.

If you want to know what an eternity is like, just begin marriage by buying everything on credit, mortgaging yourself to the limit, and you will find out!

For the first year try to get by as reasonably as possible, without buying on credit, to see how you get along. With a year or two of experience behind you, you will know the demands upon your salary and can begin projecting your acquisition goals.

Attempting to live off one salary, even though both are employed, will help financial stability. The second salary can go toward savings, or into extra house payments. Then when babies come along, the adjustment is not nearly so difficult. To cut back drastically to a considerably lower income level places stresses upon marriage at the very time of family expansion.

In the long perspective the amount of money does not matter most, rather the attitude toward money is important. Wealthy couples have just as many marital problems created by money as do the poor. Money can make people greedy, harsh, callous, unloving, and terribly suspicious. These attitudes afflict those with much as well as those with little.

In these days of recession, unemployment, inflation, and general economic insecurity, it is incumbent upon Christ-motivated people to assume a voluntarily simple standard of life, for as Jesus said, "... Life does not consist in the abundance of ... possessions" (Luke 12:15).

In-laws

A surprisingly high percentage of marriages have in-law problems. In-laws can be most difficult and irrational, catering to their own child's whims, being possessive and jealous.

On the other hand, the groom or bride likewise can be supercritical. No doubt, most marriages experience areas of irritation regarding in-laws.

Before the marriage, you as bride and groom should adjust to accepting your in-laws as parents, shortcomings and all. Expect your in-laws and your spouse to act just the way they do, to be for the present the way they are. You can help by not being judgmental.

Do not personalize your in-laws' behavior toward you, even if they seem unfair, vicious, or unfriendly. It is their problem. Take care of your own thoughts and feelings.

If at all possible, do not live in the same house with your in-laws, or even in the same neighborhood, so that you can live independently.

Try to understand your in-laws; do not expect them to be perfect; help them in every way possible; try to be a son or daughter to them; and cherish their son or daughter in their presence.

Do not show partiality to one set of parents over the other set. Give gifts that cost approximately the same. Remember special events. Plan to visit both of them frequently and about the same number of times.

Remember, your in-laws did bear and rear your spouse. They must have some nice qualities, or you would not have such a nice mate! The better you love your partner, the more likely you are to find excellent points in your in-laws.

Reflection Guide 10

1. What are the pros and cons of living together before marriage?
2. Why shouldn't engaged couples engage in sex?
3. Can sexual compatibility really be determined before marriage? Why?
4. What is the difference between *adultery* and *fornication?* Why does the Bible and why did Jesus condemn both as sinful?
5. What are the arguments for fidelity before marriage?
6. What is the greatest male motivation for marriage?
7. What are the various kinds of venereal diseases? How are they contracted primarily?
8. Is there any assurance of fidelity in marriage if there has been sexual freedom before marriage?
9. What is the major cause of marriage breakup?
10. What is the best deterrent to infidelity?

10

Sex Before Marriage

You may ask, "Should we live together before marrying? Now that we are engaged, isn't that a green light for premarital sex?"

Scores of studies indicate the extent of premarital sex participation preceding marriage. As religious and traditional influences have lessened, its practice has multiplied, with little stigma or social censure. Hollywood movies and television "soaps" have become increasingly explicit. Salable fiction seems required to have an abundance of spiced-up fornication and adultery. Commercial sales departments utilize sex appeal to advertise their products.

The Women's Liberation Movement spotlighted the traditional, hypocritical double standard, which gave men a special license for sexual freedom, while expecting women to be virgins at marriage, faithful to their husbands, willing to forgive, forget, and endure. Today's women make it clear that they require sexual fulfillment as much as men.

Among both the married and unmarried, a national preoccupation with promiscuous sexuality has swept across our nation. Sex for singles receives acceptance in many circles.

Many condone complete sexual exploration before marriage. Some males expect sex as payment for an evening out.

Young people going steady and becoming engaged often consider sexual exploration a necessary part of knowing each other and testing their love. In reality they consider sex tantamount to love. Trial marriages or live-in arrangements become increasingly common as "compatibility" tests. Open marriage and free sex now challenge the ideal of fidelity.

The normal couple faces this sex decision at some point. What should be your attitude in this regard?

How Participants Feel

A sample of varied responses by persons engaging in premarital sex follows. Some, mostly men, had positive feelings; others, mostly women, expressed negative thoughts. The most frequent positive comments were:

> "It gave me a sense of conquest . . . it was wonderful. I want it now, every time we're together."

> An engaged woman said, "I have said 'no' so many times, but there was such an inner struggle of waiting and needing it so bad that there was a physical hurt. The guilt I felt after finally saying 'yes' provided much less anguish. It was a battle I carried on for many months. I decided God would understand my needs."

> "I like it. I believe living together before marriage has helped me to know Harry. We can live together while we finish our schooling. Then when we want children we will marry."

> "It's like we were married, but we don't have all the responsibilities. We can split anytime without all the hassle."

> "I feel somewhat of an inner conflict, but my sexual experience is only with the man I plan to marry."[17]

Negative Feelings

The frequent negative comments included:

> "I feel a little guilty."

> "I felt a sense of being used, like being a whore."

"It was superficial, shallow and empty."

"I found that I felt angry at myself and resentful for sex for my own benefit."

"Even though I wanted it, I've lost respect for the other person."

"I feared rejection if I didn't go along. Now I feel it was a way of controlling me, and of gaining certain advantages."

"Now she feels she possesses me."

"Sex has short-circuited our relationship. Not enough time was allowed to elapse before it was initiated. It's basically a physical relationship."

"Communication and intimate growth are blocked by overemphasis on the physical."

A divorced woman confesses: "Premarital sex was involved before my marriage. In hindsight, I believe we were both selfish. I always felt guilty until we married. I feel now that he wanted what he wanted when he wanted it, and I wanted to please him."[18]

Prevalent Rationalizations

Testing Sexual Compatibility

The frequent pitches made included, "We're going steady, so why not have sex?" "Now we are engaged, we need to know one another. We cannot do that without experiencing sex together. That's the purpose of engagement." "I will never marry until I know from experience that we are sexually compatible."

Many have bought the argument. A divorcée states, "We had very serious sexual problems, which were the cause of the divorce, so I would never marry again without being sure that I was sexually compatible with my husband. Would you like to marry and then discover you were sexually incompatible?"

Another divorcée said, "If my husband and I had slept together when we were engaged, we would never have married. It was disastrous. I have told my children that they should find out how good their sexual adjustment is with anyone they are thinking of marrying."

Many disillusioned and disappointed men and women attribute their marriage failure to sexual incompatibility. However, illicit sexual relations cannot prove compatibility. Research verifies this conclusion: Trial marriage is not a true test.

Compatibility requires a normal situation for normal responses. Before marriage a couple carries on sexual intercourse under conditions of secrecy and fear. The psychic atmosphere is not all that of the marriage bond. Elements of anxiety, guilt, and distrust may occur. The conclusions reached in premarital sex may be totally unfair, for seldom can the atmosphere encourage the girl or the boy to perform capably. To do so requires a more normal and morally accepted atmosphere.

Furthermore, the majority of harmonious sexual relations are not achieved until months or years of unselfish adjustment, patient experimentation, and mutual understanding after the marriage consummation. Sexual compatibility roots as much in personality adjustments as it does in sexual adjustment. Sex gets better and better as one learns the art of the marriage act in the atmosphere of permanence, belonging, and social approval.

One gains little assurance in premarital sex. The physical exploration of sex can wait until the more conducive, stabilizing atmosphere of marriage. It gives couples something exciting, new, and wonderful to look forward to on the wedding night. It isn't old hat!

If You Love Me

Another argument used with persuasive skill goes like this, "You say you love me. Prove it. If you are unwilling to express your love in sex, it indicates that you do not love me." More often than not the other intends to force the girl or the boy into submission to sex, under the threat of breaking off the relationship.

Anyway, that accusation is false. Premarital sex may deny love, rather than prove it. Restraint from sex actually indicates a concern for the welfare, reputation, and wishes of the one you love. Love is unselfish and "... does not insist on its own way ..." (1 Corinthians 13:5). True love will not destroy the honor of another or violate his or her conscience or sense of values. True love has a sense of reverence for human personality and will not risk embarrassing another or compromising his or her morals. "Love is patient.... is not irritable ..." (1 Corinthians 13:4, 5), or demanding. True love will last.

As vital as sex is to a good marriage and to mental and physical health, you will not marry for sex alone. Keep sex in proper perspective as a part of a larger picture that emphasizes the quality of human interaction between you and your partner.

Ulterior Motives

More often than not, the male puts pressure on the girl for premarital sex, a normal result, since men generally are more highly sexed and easily aroused than are women. So he uses many arguments to get his way. One technique is flattery. Every girl likes to be called sweet-sounding names and to be complimented. It disarms her; she may melt and cuddle with such romantic overtures.

Or the boy can humiliate his reluctant lover by accusing her of being old-fashioned, prudish, narrow-minded, and stubborn. No girl likes these adjectives pinned upon her. They force submission. He may accuse her of being *frigid,* meaning she lacks the sex urge, making her undesirable as a mate. This fallacious conclusion is only an attempt to get his wishes.

Heavy petting, if allowed to go too far and too long, arouses sexual feelings until a girl can't say no. Both share the responsibility to avoid such intimacies. To avoid this circumstance, which the boy delights in, the girl should aim to divert thoughts and sublimate energies into other activities.

Using alcohol or drugs is a common method by which to lessen inhibitions. Girls and boys lose their powers of resistance sooner when "under the influence." Many a youth has lost virginity on a drinking spree.

Many girls have heard the line, "There is no danger if we use a contraceptive." But the record plainly proves that contraceptives sometimes fail. Furthermore there is an explosion of venereal diseases: syphilis, gonorrhea, herpes, contracted most of the time in promiscuous sex. This certainly should be a deterrent to premaritial sex.

The danger is not physical alone. Even more profound psychological scars result—guilt, resentment, loss of respect, anger—and the girl pays the most. She has more at stake by the very nature of being a woman.

"No one will ever know, so what's the difference?" What a convincing argument! Yet you will know. Your partner will know. Others may find out. And God will know. It is true, ". . . Nothing is covered that will not be revealed, or hidden that will not be known" (Matthew 10:26). "For God will bring every deed into judgment, with every secret thing, whether good or evil" (Ecclesiastes 12:14).

The Case for Fidelity

Before Marriage

Premarital sex can easily destroy the foundation for and formulation of a new marriage.

Sex acts as a primary device that drives the male toward marriage. If this is satisfied short of marriage, the male loses that basic incentive, with the frequent result of indefinite postponement of a wedding date. "Why should I get married," boasts a modern Casinova, "when I can get all the sex I want outside of marriage—and with no commitment?"

Some people are so narcissistic, selfish, and self-absorbed that they do not feel the need to be faithful; they do not really value the relationship at all, except for what they themselves get out of it. Skilled in the "on again, off again" quality of relationship, they run roughshod over others' feelings. Such people have a unique ability to manipulate others, especially through sex. They deliver a mixed message, "I love you, but I really don't love you. I love myself more, but don't go away, because I need you." Beware!

The famous Kinsey report of thirty years ago, depicting the sex habits of Americans, came to a conclusion which is still true: Men who have active sexual lives before marriage are more inclined to infidelity after marriage.

If you engage in sex before marriage, what will restrain you from having extramarital sex? What assurance will there be for fidelity in marriage if there has been sexual freedom before marriage? By engaging in premarital sex, you rationalize your actions, become skilled in the art of deception, learn to manipulate—all bad omens for an enduring marriage.

Men and women entering marriage must be conscious of the fact that the strength of commitment, personal integrity, and the interpersonal bond make the marriage work. These take time to develop and require trust.

In Marriage

Infidelity is the major cause of marriage breakups.

Even though some singles strongly advocate sexual freedom, once they marry they want and expect fidelity on the part of their partners. Only in the rarest of circumstances would a premarital understanding allow pursuit of outside sex relationships.

Given the choice between living with someone who is unfaithful and ending the marriage, most do the latter. Some retain their marriage despite this, yet the extramarital affair signals problems in the relationship and instability within the individuals.

Some psychiatrists, psychologists, and social scientists suggest that an occasional affair can be good for a marriage. They maintain it can bring personal growth, new perspective, and a new way of looking at marriage to the relationship.

This assertion is more fiction than fact. An unavoidable sense of betrayal and an inescapable hurt follow discovery.

One never completely forgets, even when one forgives, and an inkling of distrust lingers. Someone else's affair may be treated with tolerance; it becomes quite another thing when betrayal hits at home. Infidelity, rather than enriching a marriage, probably obliterates the real closeness of two hearts.

Open marriage and sexual freedom may work for those husbands and wives who do not care too much for each other or where the personalities of both preclude a permanent commitment with another. Some may enjoy marriage without faithful intimacy or consistent responsibility. Most people find the concept of marital fidelity desirable and essential.

The Best Deterrent

The best deterrent to infidelity is religious faith and practice. Though this does not guarantee enduring marriage, percentage wise, fewer divorces result among actively involved church people. Religious faith and life nurture the attitudes and life practices that form the cement of human relationships. Where God lives in the human mind and heart, loyalty, unselfishness, forgiveness, and consideration also exist. A life active in service to others results in greater joy, satisfaction, and compassion. The couple that partakes of fellowship of the church should face fewer romantic triangles. Friends with similar life purposes and high moral standards are found. Constant reminders of ideals and biblical teaching provide challenges for growth. The mental catharsis from the sacraments and the prayers in regular worship experiences undergird harmonious marriage. There is preventive power in religious faith.

Venereal Disease

There are three main types of venereal disease—syphilis, gonorrhea, and herpes. They are caused by bacilli and only rarely caused by anything but direct contact with an infected person. All three exist in epidemic proportions in America and can cause serious harm if treatment is delayed.

Promiscuous sex spreads these maladies. The best preventive, therefore, is reserving intercourse for marriage, with one partner who has been medically checked.

The person who suspects that he or she might have contracted one of the diseases should consult a doctor immediately and be perfectly honest and frank. Early diagnosis and thorough treatment may save untold suffering, not only for the person, but for his or her innocent party in marriage and the future offspring.

Reflection Guide 11

1. On what date do you wish to be married? what hour of the day?
2. Where will the wedding be held?
3. Who will be in the wedding party?
4. Who will officiate at the ceremony? Have you called him for a planning conference?
5. What music will be used? what musicians? What are the church's policies regarding procedures, participants, music, photographers, and fees?
6. Where will you hold the rehearsal? Will you have a rehearsal dinner?
7. Where will the reception be held?
8. Will pictures be taken following the ceremony?
9. What florist will you use? When will the chancel be decorated?
10. When will you arrange to get your wedding license?

11

Planning the Wedding

Preferably only after several premarital counseling sessions would the details of planning the wedding proceed. This gives time for better preparation, more objective decision making, and making necessary adjustments.

Choosing the Place

Considering the basic religious character of the marriage commitment, the most appropriate scene for the ceremony is in a church sanctuary or chapel. The marriage ceremony is essentially a God-centered worship service. Marriage partners make vows to Him as well as to each other. Couples with this dimension should choose the church, not for its roominess or because it will better show off the wedding gown, or because the church will photograph better, but because it is conducive to worship. A wedding is not a performance or a modeling of ornamental attire. Rather, the sanctuary chancel contains symbols of religious heritage and the presence of the Unseen Guest. It has a sacred atmosphere and the joyous hope, faith, and love that marriage celebrates.

Some couples have home weddings for an intimate, family feeling. Others choose a garden. Some, straining for the unusual or unforgettable, have been married in such places as mountaintops or a mutually enjoyed scenic spot. Exhibitionists have been known to marry in an airplane or at a race track or athletic field or in a nightclub or bar. For the latter, it is best not to invite a clergyman to compromise his convictions for such a flippant approach. Others may choose a civil ceremony, which is done in the office or courtroom of the civil official or in the home of the bride.

The Bride's Church

The wedding traditionally is held in the bride's church, in her hometown. Only occasionally does the wedding take place in the groom's hometown or church. Customarily the bride has the prerogative to make this decision.

If she has been away from home, attending school or working, or if her family has moved to another community so she has few ties or acquaintances there, she may choose to be married at the university chapel or in the city where she works.

Who Will Do the Ceremony?

Legally one may have a civil ceremony or a religious one. If you choose a religious ceremony, the bride's current home-church pastor has the right to perform it. One of the senior minister's significant roles is counseling couples and performing marriages. If the bride or groom has a relative or close friend who is a clergyman, whom they wish to perform the service, it is permissable, as long as the couple makes arrangements for premarital counseling. The ceremony takes only twenty to thirty minutes, but the significance of marriage and its deeper implications require counseling, preferably lasting for at least three sessions. Even when a relative or friend conducts the counseling and ceremony, the minister of the local church should be involved. Occasionally the bride's and groom's minister share the ceremony, with the groom's minister assisting.

Usually a former minister should not be asked to return to a former parish to perform a ceremony. In events such as weddings, the present minister receives the opportunity to minister to his people and to establish lasting pastoral relationships. A minister who has gone from the field and returns for a wedding will be gone again without establishing the continuing professional pastoral relationship. The couple may thus shortchange themselves. Furthermore, a clergyman returning to his former field of service to perform pastoral responsibilities violates the ministerial code of ethics, unless he does so with the invitation of the current minister or in unusual circumstances that alter the rule.

Couples wishing to have a civil ceremony should choose a justice of the peace or a county or district judge who is on duty when the proper legal forms are acquired.

Initial Planning Conference With Minister

The wedding plans begin with a conference with the minister, at least twelve weeks in advance of the wedding date. You will want to hold this conference before the date and place are determined or announced. Assuming that a place and a clergyman are available and finding that they are not can cause much awkwardness.

The bride and the groom, their families, and the minister should mutually negotiate the date. The availability of the minister and the church can be easiest accomplished in the first planning conference with the minister, discussing the various options, then deciding on the date, reserving the facilities needed, and confirming the minister's schedule.

Information Needed

The bride will fill out a form with as much information as possible at this first conference. The following shows the kind of information needed:

Wedding Information[19]

Bride's full name _____

    Address _____ Phone _____

    Member of what church? _____

Bride's mother _____

    Address _____

Bride's father _____

    Address _____

Groom's full name _____

    Address _____

Groom's mother _____

    Address _____

Groom's father _____

    Address _____

Maid of honor _____

Best man _____

Male attendants: Female attendants:

_____   _____

_____   _____

_____   _____

Ring bearer: Flower girl:

_____   _____

Ushers: Candlelighters:

_____   _____

_____   _____

_____   _____

Communion at end of service?   Yes _____ No _____

Memory candle to be used?   Yes _____ No _____

Organist: _____

Singer: _____

Songs to be sung: _____

_____

Will this be a double-ring ceremony? _____

Will there be a prie-dieu (kneeling rail)? _____

Number of persons invited to wedding ceremony _____

What persons will dress at church? _____

Will dress be formal or informal? _____

Will there be a reception? _____ Where held? _____

Person in charge of reception: _____
  Address and phone _____

Persons assisting at reception table: _____

_____

Number invited to reception: _____

Do you understand the church's policy regarding use of
  alcoholic beverages? _____

Photographer _____

Will you see that he knows the church's policy regarding
  picture taking? _____

Special requests for minister: _____

_____

Date of wedding: _____ Time: _____

Date of rehearsal: _____ Time: _____

Is there a rehearsal dinner? _____ Time: _____

Who is the florist? _____
  Address and phone: _____

Please check: ____ Flowers will be picked up after wedding.

           ____ Flowers will be picked up after Sunday
                worship.

           ____ Flowers are to be taken to homebound
                members of church after the Sunday-
                morning service.

Do you understand the policy on fees? _____

What will your home address be after marriage? _____

_____

Decorations

Keep decorations for a church wedding simple and to a
minimum. The church symbolism provides an adequate atmosphere without elaborate, ornamental amenities. Each congre-

gation will have its own policies in this regard, and they should be strictly abided by.

Photographer

Choose the photographer carefully, because he can destroy the solemnity of the occasion if he is too commercial.

Most churches will have a policy of no pictures taken during the ceremony, because it is a worship service, not for display. Experience has taught that if the wedding party will be fully attired thirty minutes prior to the procession time, the photographer can make pre-wedding pictures of the bride and her entourage and the groom and his attendants in the rooms where they are waiting.

Occasionally, a photographer asks all participants to come dressed for pictures an hour or two before wedding time. Vigorously resist this, because it causes a long wait for the wedding party, which jeopardizes the freshness of their dress, distracts from the approaching ceremony, and often results in irritations caused by impatience and tensions.

After the ceremony the wedding party can immediately come back by a side chancel door, re-posing for seven or eight different photos. Again time is important, especially if the reception immediately follows the service. Give the photographer a list of the shots desired.

Costs

The costs of a wedding can be enormous or quite modest, depending upon the desires of the bride and her parents' resources. The major expense items center on the purchase of the wedding gown, attendant's apparel (customarily furnished by the attendants), floral arrangements, photography, wedding dinner, reception, and honeymoon.

Most churches, wishing not to discourage persons from marrying in the sanctuary or chapel, will hold their costs to a minimum, including services of organist, custodians, and clergyman. Persons who are not members of the particular congregation will usually pay a rental or utility charge not expected from members. A reception in the church's parlor entails an additional cost, generally far under the cost by a similar commercial facility. If the church ladies prepare the reception, again it is considerably less than a catered reception. Many churches, however, have a rule against serving alcoholic beverages.

Some clergymen have no set fee for their services; however, they probably spend more time than anyone else in the preparation, including the counseling sessions, rehearsal, rehearsal dinner, wedding, and reception. They should be paid accordingly. Some clergymen consider the wedding responsibility as part of their church's ministry and give their fees to the church's library or scholarship fund.

Financial Obligations of the Bride

Since the major portion of the wedding expenses falls on the bride's family, the sensible girl does not insist that her family go into near bankruptcy with an elaborate wedding. She will use simplicity in decorations, dress, and accompanying arrangements. The bride's financial responsibilities are as follows:

Engraving of invitations and announcements
Mailing of invitations, cards, and announcements
Transportation for attendants to and from church
Hotel bills for her attendants, when bride's parents cannot accommodate them
Organist
Soloist
Rental of church and custodial fees
Wedding reception
Groom's ring
Bride's trousseau

Wedding photographs
Gifts to the bridesmaids and maid (or matron) of honor
Bridesmaids' flowers
Church decorations
Gift to groom

FINANCIAL OBLIGATIONS OF THE GROOM

Marriage license
Bride's ring
Bachelor dinner (optional)
Rehearsal dinner
Gift to bride
Bride's flowers
Transportation for male attendants to and from church
Clergyman's fee
Corsages for mothers of the bride and the groom
Boutonnieres for best man, ushers, groomsmen, groom's father, and the minister
Gifts to male attendants and ushers
Ties and gloves for attendants (optional)
Hotel bill for his attendants from out of town
Wedding trip[20]

Wedding Music

The selection of music for the wedding should be fitting for a Christian service, maintaining the dignity, meaning, and spiritual basis of marriage. Use God-directed music rather than subjective, romantic music. Some couples make the mistake of choosing their favorite popular or show tunes. Have these, if they must be used, at the rehearsal dinner or at the reception.

Most churches establish a music policy. The minister may submit a listing of what his church considers acceptable wedding music, from which the bride and groom may choose. Some ministers are rigid in this regard; others retain some flexibility.

Many churches omit the much used traditional Wagner and Mendelssohn wedding marches from marriage services and replace them with Trumpet Tune in D or Trumpet Voluntary in D by Purcell or great processional hymns. The reasons are convincing. "Here comes the bride," from Wagner's *Lohengrin,* was never intended for church use. In the opera, this excerpt occurs when the bride and groom enter the bridal chamber. In the play, filled with sensuality, the groom murders a rival, and he abandons his wife forever. With this origin, many consider the music inappropriate for a Christian wedding.

The wedding organist should be the regular church organist or assistant organist, since they are familiar with the church's instrument, the church's repertoire, and the minister's routine. If the bride desires a friend to play, she should obtain approval from the church's music committee or minister or organist.

Vocal music, when desired, may be by the choir, or ensemble, or a soloist. If a couple chooses a vocal soloist, great care should be exercised to have someone with ability and experience and the proper repertoire to make a positive contribution.

Rehearsal

Usually the presiding minister prefers to conduct the rehearsal, so that all the details are adequately explained for an orderly wedding. Ministers of large parishes often have an assistant or hostess who does this. Some couples employ a professional wedding consultant or have the florist do it. An orderly, thorough rehearsal will make sure everyone, especially the bride and groom and ushers, understands the responsibilities for each.

The Rehearsal Dinner

An increasing number of people hold a dinner following the rehearsal, for all persons in the wedding party. In this event the rehearsal should be conducted at 6:00 P.M. or 6:30 P.M., allowing an hour for the rehearsal.

The groom or his parents will make the necessary arrangements for the dinner, send written invitations, and pay for the dinner.

During the dinner, the attendants, parents, and other family and friends will want to extend toasts to the bride and groom. Usually the bride and groom also express appreciation to their family and friends for their participation and present each attendant with a modest gift. The couple may also give each other gifts.

The Reception

The reception may consist of a wedding cake; a groom's cake, if you wish; with punch and coffee, nuts and mints. This is quite adequate. However, some serve a variety of finger food as well. Occasionally a couple plans a full wedding dinner.

The bride and groom may circulate among the guests or form a receiving line. If a receiving line is formed, it will usually include the following, in order:

Bride's mother
Groom's mother
Bride's father (optional)
Groom's father (optional)
Bride
Groom
Maid of honor
Best man
Bridesmaids (optional)
Groomsmen (optional)

Preparation Schedule

Checklist for Bride and Groom

The following list could be used by the bride from the time of the first conference:

Twelfth Week Before Wedding

1. Have conference with minister to arrange day and time.
2. Make reservation for church use for both wedding and reception. If reception is not in a church, you may have to make earlier arrangements.
3. Learn the policy of the church regarding costs, decorations, etc.
4. Schedule at least two or three more premarital counseling sessions.
5. Make arrangements with organist, other musicians, and primary attendants.
6. Read through a wedding planning book.

Eleventh Week Before Wedding

1. Make out wedding invitation list.
2. Make out reception list.
3. Make out announcement list.
4. Order invitations and announcements.
5. Have conference with the caterer.

Tenth Week Before Wedding

1. Select and get commitments from members of the wedding party.
2. Choose general color scheme and flowers.

Ninth and Eighth Weeks Before Wedding

1. Order or begin making wedding dress.
2. Arrange date, time, and place of rehearsal dinner.
3. Select china, glassware, and silver patterns.

Seventh Week Before Wedding

1. Make arrangements with florist.
2. Make arrangements with photographer.
3. Order printed napkins, etc., for reception.
4. Have conference with minister.

Sixth Week Before Wedding
1. Pick out gifts for attendants.
2. Arrange for housing of guests from out of town.
3. Read literature recommended by the minister.
4. Buy wedding rings.

Fifth Week Before the Wedding
1. Buy going-away clothes.
2. Make honeymoon trip reservations.

Fourth Week Before Wedding
1. Have conference with physician.
2. Have blood test.
3. Recheck with all attendants to confirm that they will be present.
4. Send out invitations to wedding and to rehearsal dinner.
5. Submit a release to newspaper of announced wedding plans.

Third Week Before Wedding
1. Give a bridesmaids' luncheon or tea.

Second Week Before Wedding
1. Get license.
2. Have conference with minister.
3. Pose a bride's picture for newspaper.

Last Week Before Wedding
1. Remind all participants regarding rehearsal attendance.
2. Have newspaper release ready.
3. Arrange for announcements to be mailed the day of the ceremony.[21]

Reflection Guide 12

1. Why is a marriage ceremony important?
2. Have you read through a meaningful Christian wedding ceremony?
3. Do you understand why most weddings are conducted in the church?
4. Do you understand why the father gives consent to the marriage?
5. Why are witnesses required by the state?
6. Is the marriage commitment unconditional?
7. Why is marriage not considered a contract?
8. How can money help or hinder a marriage?
9. Why is it recommended that there be a double-ring ceremony?
10. What does God join together? What has He put asunder?

12

The Marriage Ceremony

Some contemporary couples have questioned, "Why is a ceremony necessary? We are just as much married in our hearts whether or not we have a wedding. The certificate is just a piece of paper."

Ceremonies are important in life to make public what we feel in our hearts, to openly declare our commitments, without reservation or shame, to celebrate significant occasions with our families and friends. The wedding ceremony is perhaps the most meaningful ritual of all.

"Young people who are hesitant to seal their union legally reveal that their commitment to one another is not total. Marriage licenses and ceremonies are not only legal formalities, they are also symbols of responsibility."[22]

For example, two people just living together have no obligations to each other when the tax forms come up for audit or the other becomes involved in a car accident and a legal suit. Persons holding a marriage license do have such responsibility. Commitment to a marriage involves accepting that public responsibility.

Look carefully at the ceremony itself. There are many forms, both civil and religious, traditional and contemporary, Protestant and Roman Catholic. Most ceremonies contain the following phrases, if not verbatim, at least in concept.

"We Are Gathered Together in the Sight of God" God's law, not the law of the state, gives two people the right to live together. They should seek His approval for the union. The couple makes their vows in His presence. For that reason the church is the most appropriate place for such a service. God is the primary guest, the only one whom an usher does not greet and lead to a pew, the only guest mentioned by the leader in worship. The wedding functions not as a performance for the guests, but as a religious worship service directed to God.

"In the Presence of These Witnesses" Marriage is not a private affair, designed to provide personal pleasure for two people pooling their selfish interests. It has a public character, therefore the ceremony should not take place in secrecy or by elopement. This contradicts the basic idea of marriage.

Because your union may produce children, society has a stake in your marriage. The offspring may become a burden to or a strength in the community. When the father presents the bride for marriage, symbolically he acts on behalf of both families and the entire community to give responsible approval to the union.

Publicly the groom declares that he has chosen this one girl to be his life companion, so all other relationships are terminated. He vocalizes his intentions and his promises of fidelity before God. The bride does likewise. The joy for bride and groom increases with their sharing it with others. The goodwill of others inspires and encourages.

"Not to Be Entered Into Unadvisedly or Lightly" Do not undertake marriage without counsel. Hurrying into a relationship without adequate advice before plans are made is extremely risky and ill-advised. I recommend a minimum of three counseling sessions with an experienced counselor.

The state itself has established some mandatory guidelines: You must be free from certain diseases; you must be of certain age or have consent of parents; you have to buy a license and have it recorded to make the relationship public. You must not be in too great a rush, so the state requires a waiting time between blood tests, purchasing the license, and getting married.

Like it or not, when you marry, you become part of an entire clan. Your family knows better than you do who will fit in, so their counsel needs to be sought.

The church is an expert in marriage counseling, because its theology describes marriage as not only a meeting of bodies, but a blending of souls. From observation the church knows the dangers of marriage between persons too different in ages, interests, religious views, and traditions.

"WILL YOU TAKE THIS WOMAN?"   You, as a man, never totally know how a woman feels or thinks. As Dr. Kenneth H. Foreman says, "You are about to share life with a person to whom, in many ways, you must be an everlasting stranger.... In little ways she will puzzle you.... Being a woman, she will be different from you, which will by turns intoxicate and madden you, bring you to despair and amazement and delight."[23] A woman will often be concerned over trifles and indifferent to much that makes up a man's world.

If you have chosen a good wife, you will have her eyes through which to see mankind in a new light and her heart through which to feel life's most precious treasures.

Will you take this woman? Marriage is voluntary. It involves the acceptance of a bond. Absolute freedom or undisciplined free expression no longer have a place in your lives. Free love and open marriage contradict the true meaning of marriage. In marrying you commit yourself exclusively to this woman and rule out the possibility of love for other women.

"WILL YOU TAKE THIS MAN?"   Before you think *who* he is, think *what* he is. You are about to enter into the closest, most intimate life-sharing relationship with a person; however, since you are a woman and he is a man, you will never completely understand him. You may think you know him, but you do not; only marriage can teach you, and then only in part. The hopes and thoughts of your man you can never completely imagine nor fully share. His drives and responses you will experience but never completely comprehend. He may not sympathize with your most serious difficulties, nor vocalize his admiration for your most recognized virtues. He may be as changeable as the wind, yet as strong as steel; as fickle as a teenager, yet as sturdy as the Rock of Gibraltar.

"FOR BETTER, FOR WORSE" Marriage is a commitment, in contrast to being a contract. A contract would contain an escape clause. Commitment is unconditional. One does not enter into true marriage with fingers crossed. The ceremony is intensely realistic, rather than sentimental, for it recognizes the pitfalls in advance.

The commitment is "for better, for worse." Some never expect the "worse," so they start with a halfway commitment—"for better." Every person has some strange quirks, oddities, and weird habits. You may not even notice them until you are married; then they become annoying, like sand in a shoe. The accumulation of little things can explode into a huge incident. The art of happy marriage means getting along with your mate in spite of peculiarities and utilizing them for a close bond. Just remember, you have some oddities, too!

Do not assume the words of the musical *Guys and Dolls* that say, "Marry the man today and change his ways tomorrow." Marriage rarely, if ever, makes a poor relationship better. You may recognize the other person as not perfect, but feel you can change all that. If not altered before marriage, seldom are drinking habits, bad temper, promiscuity, indifference to the church, or annoying habits conquered after marriage. People can and do change for the better after marriage, but not without considerable pain.

Marriage is not always "for better." There will be disappointments, disillusionments, grief, sorrows, difficulties, and unpleasant experiences that would not happen apart from marriage. When you stand before God and the witnesses, promising to take this man or this woman "for better, for worse," you take this person through the pleasant and the unpleasant, the light and the dark, the good and the bad, no matter what.

"FOR RICHER, FOR POORER"   A common thing like the quantity of money you have can shatter marriage.

Perhaps you believe that becoming wealthy could be the finest thing that could happen in your marriage. You sincerely hope to become rich. However, the Bible considers wealth as a chief risk in life.

If you grow rich by your own efforts, you have to work longer hours and spend more time away from home, the perils of which place a great strain upon your marriage.

If you have inherited wealth, then the temptation is to spend carelessly, become selfish, lazy, and callous to human need. It may invite disaster to your marriage.

Climbing to a higher salary bracket may mean another set of friends. Many a man rising into the higher section of society has found his wife not quite "good enough" anymore. Or many a woman accepted her husband when they were poor because he was the best she could get at the time. Once they went into a higher social set, she left him for another whom she could never have attracted in her poverty.

Is your love strong enough to go through the trials of growing richer?

"IN SICKNESS AND IN HEALTH"   Sickness is not just a possibility; it is a certainty. Whatever else may stay the same, your state of health will inevitably change. Sooner or later you will know pain, disease, and diminishing health.

Nothing so strains marriage loyalty as a premature break-down in health, leaving one unable to function normally. Sickness alters personality. Being isolated from the outside world may lead to abnormal paranoia, depression, resentment, or hostility. It is not uncommon for the sick person to feel neglected by an unsympathetic mate, accuse him or her of all kinds of fallacious irresponsibility and lack of love. It would be well if one mate did not take as personal what the other may say or do when ill, for he or she may not be showing the real self.

Do all that you can to keep illness away. Right eating habits, sufficient food, proper sleep, adequate exercise, frequent physical checkups, congenial relationships, personal religious faith, and a merry heart are the best antidotes to declining health. You can do more than anyone else to keep your mate healthy. Then, whatever illnesses may come, together you can accept and bear what you must.

"So LONG AS YOU BOTH SHALL LIVE ... FROM THIS DAY FORWARD" You are starting out in the most daring of human adventures. The Christian ideal of marriage calls for nothing less than the union of one man and one woman for a lifetime: "until death shall part us."

It is a permanent relationship. You cannot view it as a commitment just until the present mood wears off or until harsh words erupt between you or until poverty overtakes you or until you can find a more congenial partner or until trouble becomes unbearable or old age creeps upon you.

The commitment is "for so long as you both shall live." Many people in America enter marriage with a temporary mentality. "If things don't work out, we will split," they say. This does not describe the Christian concept of marriage. Married life begun so flimsily will break up over trifles, when moods change and irritations become exaggerated into mountains.

"WHOM GOD HAS JOINED TOGETHER, LET NO ONE PUT ASUNDER" God has joined together sex and love, marriage and in-

tercourse. Let no man put them asunder. God has joined together fidelity and happiness. When we try to separate them,
we run into trouble.

These words are true in reverse. What God has put asunder,
let no man put together. God has put asunder the license of im-
moral indulgence from enduring satisfactions in life. God has
put asunder selfishness and marriage. A great deal of marital
unhappiness and divorce has come from efforts to join together
what God has separated.

In a true marriage husband and wife are so united and spiri-
tually infused that neither one is any longer a separate entity.
One does not lose his or her total individuality, yet each
achieves full personality by becoming one with the other. The
sentiments and affections of one become the sentiments and affections of the other—so much so that children and friends
find it hard to think of one without the other. Indeed, each will
wonder what they could possibly have been before their lives
were joined into one. That kind of unity is impossible except
by the cement of God's Spirit.

Reflection Guide 13

1. Have you had adequate sex education?
2. What is the primary source of your information about sex?
3. What do you think are the God-designed purposes of sex?
4. Do you understand the differences in male and female arousal?
5. Have you both read a reliable sex manual, providing helpful information regarding how to achieve mutual fulfillment in intercourse?
6. Can a couple expect mutual fulfillment every time?
7. How often should you have sex?
8. Should the wife give in to her husband every time he desires when she does not? or vice versa?
9. What are the periods and purposes of restraint?
10. How can sex be used to God's glory? how misused to God's condemnation?

13

Bedroom Knowledge for Beginners

Sources of Sex Knowledge

What is the source of your sex knowledge? Most people come to marriage with much inadequate, inaccurate, or corrupted sex information. Couples assume they know all about it, because since their childhood, sex has saturated X-rated movies, contemporary literature, and most commercials. Explicit pornography has been available, neighborhood gangs and fraternities constantly discuss sex, classes in public schools have dealt with the subject. Red-light districts have exposed lurid scenes. Seldom does primary sex information come predominantly from the parents. In fact, most youths embarrass their parents with the extent of their sex knowledge.

The difficulty concerns the quality of the knowledge. So much is unhealthy, smutlike garbage from the alleys and streets, influenced by Hollywood immorality.

This chapter purposes to give sex knowledge from a Christian perspective, intended to make the experience beautiful.

God Designed

Sex can be cheap, distorted, misused, and corrupted, or it can be beautiful, exciting, and joyful, as God intended. Sex within marriage is a sacred experience.

God in His infinite wisdom designed us male and female. Dr. Henry Brandt, a Christian psychologist, reminds us, "God created all parts of the human body. He did not create some parts good and some bad; He created them all good, for when He had finished His creation, He looked at it and said, 'It is all very good' " (Gen. 1:31).[24] Intrinsically there is nothing dirty, sinful, or corrupting in the sexual act itself. What we do with sex may create sin.

The Purposes of Sex

Sex fulfills four positive purposes within healthy marriage.[25] Each of these God-designed purposes enhances the sacred dimension of the marriage act.

The Unifying Function

Sex within marriage acts as a unifying factor. Two lives blend into one as the waters of confluent streams mingle. Satisfying sex bridges the separateness of husband and wife. It is a beautiful way of expressing emotional connectedness.

The physical-emotional-spiritual joining in sex is God's design for merging two inner worlds. Joining bodies and spirits functions as therapy for inner loneliness and isolation.

Sexual intimacy is rooted in a biological drive. This physiological basis of sexual attraction exists in all animals. But in the human being there develops a unique blend of the physiological and the psychological. The physical need for release of sexual desire intertwines with a variety of psychological needs: for the security and warmth of body closeness and stroking; for feeling loved, cared about, and cherished; for affirmation of one's sexuality. Both the joys and the problems of sex center almost entirely in the psychological-emotional area, rather than in the physical aspect of the relationship.

Sex without a love relationship is shallow. Sex feeds love and is fed by love. As W. Clark Ellzery says, "If sex is sought on the animal level, nothing but animal returns can be expected."[26] Satisfying of the personality hunger is equally important as the physical hunger.

Marriage plays a vital role in the uniting of these two forms of intimacy—physical and psychological.

Reuel Howe in a *Reader's Digest* article on the subject writes:

> Male and female were not created to exist separately. Woman was made to complete man; and man, woman—anatomically, biologically, emotionally, mentally, and spiritually. The power of the sex drive springs from the longings of the incomplete being for completion. A divided creation consequently suffers, longing for union and fulfillment ... The union sought, however, is more than sexual. It is a longing for a special union of which the sexual is but a part and not the whole.[27]

The Enjoyment of Life Together

Sex in marriage enhances the enjoyment of life together. God intended it to be pleasurable; it is not sinful to enjoy it. There is something wrong if both husband and wife do not enjoy it.

A satisfying sex experience releases tensions, renews tired spirits, and offsets the heartaches and failures of human existence. Engaging in sex helps both individuals drop the load of adult responsibilities and lets the inner child play. Sex gives wings to the hearts of husband and wife, amid the pressures and worries of daily life. Together in sex they celebrate the pleasures of life.

Edrita Fried says, "A sexual experience resembles a short vacation trip. A lover comes back to everyday conditions as a traveler returns home. Like the returning traveler, he reacts more vividly and sharply to the accustomed environment."[28]

Completing Your Identity

Sex strengthens and completes your identity. Each of you brings a degree of unfinished identity to marriage. One's own identity is increased by joining worlds with a person of the opposite sex. As the Clinebells put it, "The femaleness of a wife brings out the maleness in the husband, and vice versa."[29] This mutual heightening of femininity and masculinity brings zest to a marriage. Each of us needs to have our sexuality affirmed and rejoiced in by our mate. Do not withhold comments such as, "I really enjoyed that," or, "You made last night heavenly," or, "You're terrific in bed," for they will enhance your sexual identities.

Parenting

The basic God-designed purpose of sex in marriage is reproduction. Only a thousandth or less of sex relationships in marriage have anything to do with reproduction, yet no reproduction takes place without sex.

The late Dr. Paul Tillich observed that "the Biblical idea that mates become 'one flesh' goes beyond intercourse in its fullest expression. Two persons literally become 'one flesh' in the joining of genes in their children. Sexual intercourse only begins the reproductive process."[30] The process of parenting is a lifelong experience, for one is always a parent once the process begins.

Bedroom Intimacy

Intercourse is the most intimate human relationship. It is the blending, for one brief period, of two bodies and two personalities into one heightened by the most ecstatic sensation accompanied by warmest love and deepest trust. Satisfying sex is the basis for harmonious marriage.[31]

Young couples often believe that because they are "in love," they can go to bed on the night of their wedding and have a glorious experience.

Learning the art of lovemaking takes time and practice within a secure relationship, which a premarital relationship is not. Many feelings have to be worked through, such as embarrassment, tension, guilt, fear, apprehension, and misconceptions. Frequently the first experience is painful for the wife. Seldom is it mutually satisfying. The couple must realize that just because they have a disappointing initial sex experience, it does not consign them to a lifetime of sexual frustration.

Sexual adjustment problems are frequent and require patience, experimentation, open communication, and complete cooperation.

Every couple should work out mutually satisfying procedures and techniques. No set patterns fit everyone.

The sex act should be unhurried, relaxed, enjoyable, and not forced. Complete fulfillment cannot be expected immediately or every time, however, this does not mean the couple should view their sex life as a failure.

Though the following paragraphs emphasize techniques for the beginning couple, it needs to be remembered that the attitudes of caring and sharing, of warmth and tenderness, plus gestures and words of endearment and intimacy play an equally important part in satisfying sex.

Mutually satisfying intercourse does not happen automatically. It must be consciously worked at and experimented with until each knows what arouses the other the best and what each finds enjoyable.

Love Play

Every act of intercourse should be preceded by a period of love play to build desire and passion to the point of readiness for intercourse.

A man's sexual responses are different and his arousal faster.

He can achieve an erection instantaneously. A kiss, the sight of a nude or partially nude woman, the thoughts of sex, and he usually becomes aroused. As soon as an erection occurs, he is ready for intercourse. Because erection comes easily and ejaculation quickly, a man can achieve a measure of satisfaction even with an unresponsive or unaroused wife.

A woman's responses are usually much slower to arouse. Most women require some love play to arouse them sufficiently to an active role in intercourse, but all women require some foreplay to stimulate their passion to an orgasm pitch. Caressing and petting prepare a woman for this. Because a woman reacts slowly, she depends upon the man for sexual satisfaction. She need not remain passive, letting him do all the lovemaking. She should share in the kissing and caressing of her husband and in body and verbal language.

The wife should never hesitate to initiate love play when she desires sex, though usually the husband initiates it because his desires are usually more frequent and stronger.

Proper Framework

A couple needs a proper emotional and situational framework for sex to achieve satisfaction. You do not have to be "in the mood for sex" before your partner stirs your interest, but you do need a cheerful disposition. Emotional disturbances thoroughly block the sexual apparatus. Depression, anger, fear, tension, irritation, or ill feeling makes successful sexual communion nearly impossible.

When you feel very close to each other, in the privacy of your home you respond to your spouse's feelings, and he or she responds to yours, building anticipation and cooperation.

Conditioning

Sexual desire is not spontaneous. Conditioning plays a big part in sexual allurement. Some couples, especially women, find that reading rather explicit descriptions of sex experiences in novels, or viewing a romantic movie, or TV soap opera stirs the chords of desire. The scents of a favorite perfume, the allurement of nightdress, the strains of romantic background music all subtly stir sex urges and excitement.

Preliminary Touching

Even though vision, hearing, and smelling contribute to sexual excitement, the buildup of passion requires contact and caressing. Gentle stroking and caressing, made even gentler by moisture, build excitement best.

What you caress and how you caress have much to do with sex buildup. Using the palms of your hands, the tips of your fingers, the moist surfaces of your lips, and the tip of your tongue builds your own excitement as well as your partner's.

Women depend upon the early passion-building caresses on parts of the body such as the hair, the shoulders, back, upper arms, breasts, and inner thighs. Sexual sensitivity in men centers more in the back of the neck and in thighs and has less importance, in comparison, than with the female.

Genital Caressing

Finally, when the wife is ready, the sex-play activity will center in the genital zone. This will excite her ardor even further. Both husband and wife can engage in this form of normal sex play. Remember that the key to the woman's ability to reach climax is triggered by clitoral massaging. Some women find it necessary to reach an initial orgasm in this manner, before intercourse begins, after which they may have multiple orgasms.

Deviate Forms

Many forms of caressing and intercourse to which many people have built-in inhibitions, have received considerable publicity. They feel particularly repelled by mouth-to-genital forms of foreplay. Others may find it sexually exciting. Perhaps you or your spouse cannot force yourself to these acts without intense emotional reaction. If so, neither the husband nor wife should insist upon the practice. It is best not to force the issue or the practice. All should be done within the limits of sanitation, propriety, and personal comfort.

Intercourse and Orgasm

The act of intercourse consists of the insertion of the erect penis into the expectant vagina and the thrusting movements leading to greater intensity culminating in the orgasm. The muscles in the body contract involuntarily and sometimes violently.

Orgasms vary in intensity. Some are slight, while others are very strong. The sensation of orgasm centers in the gland of the male penis and in the female's clitoris and perhaps in the vagina.

In men orgasm induces ejaculation of sperm, propelling the male semen into the female. Women experience no ejaculation, though involuntary spasmodic muscle contractions occur within the vagina.

Strive for the ideal of complete satisfaction for both partners, culminating in simultaneous orgasm. This cannot always be achieved. With proper patience, study, experimentation, and cooperation, mutual satisfaction can be reached frequently.

Adjustments for Mutual Satisfaction

Sex orgasm is not the total point of lovemaking. If she fails to attain orgasm every time, a woman should not consider the situation hopeless. Female orgasm, elusive, complex, and easily sidetracked by noise, disruption, or fear, need not be achieved every time. A woman *can* even enjoy intercourse without orgasm (some never experience one), but it is important for a loving couple to experiment and adjust until the woman does climax, at least part of the time.

If a couple will not work this out, it may become a hang-up, and the woman may feel she lacks femininity. She may experience a distaste for sex and dislike frequent relations. But this need not happen.

Take Ample Time

If a woman seldom has an orgasm, it is usually for several reasons. One may be that lovemaking has been too rushed to allow ample time for her to reach a climax. The husband must wait for his wife's erotic nature to blossom. This takes patience and self-control.

Vary Positions

Experimentation with positions of intercourse may help, so the penis can contact the clitoris with each stroke. Among the many positions are: the man over the woman, the woman above the man, the side-by-side position, the rear-entry position, the kneeling position, the sitting position.

There are other variations of these basic positions. Never hesitate to experiment. Anything that pleases the couple to bring fuller satisfaction is perfectly proper, right, and good.

Frigidity

The old Victorian view was that "nice" women never had sex desire and no woman was capable of real sex pleasure and satisfaction. Some of these views still persist. However, nearly all women have a sex impulse. If they do not, it is extremely damaging to marriage. This is what is usually meant by *frigidity*, "no desire for sex."

Two types of frigidity—physical and psychological—exist. Hormone deficiencies, glandular disturbances, or other physical problems cause physical frigidity and can be helped by medicinal treatment. Psychological frigidity usually results from false conceptions of marital relations, lack of sexual education, embarrassment, fear, or the overbearing treatment of an inexperienced, selfish, or ill-informed husband.

Frequency

No hard-and-fast rule exists for frequency of intercourse. Each couple must determine what is comfortable for both parties. Recent studies indicate that habits vary, ranging from several times daily to once or twice monthly.

Situations will have a strong effect on sex. Newly married couples usually have intercourse more frequently than others. A woman who is not consistently satisfied will want sex less often. Frequent disappointments may turn her completely away from copulation.

The question of frequency must be dealt with with consideration on both parts. Just because a wife cannot respond with orgasm, a couple should not eliminate sexual activity. But every husband should be thoughtful in his demands, to the extent of curbing his urges that arise at inconvenient times. Even a wife who enjoys most sexual episodes resents advances while she dresses for a party or cooks a meal or cleans house. She does not want to be kept up all night by having a late sex rendezvous. On the other hand, no wife should restrain her husband's passion for days on end, even when she is not in the mood. In allowing the tensions and burdens of the day to discourage her cooperation, his sex hungers will not be fed at home, and he may satisfy them elsewhere, or it may result in a dull and conflict-ridden sex life. As he indulges his desires and shares his feelings in marriage, his wife will grow in ardor. The hard-to-arouse wife should recognize that willing sexual indulgence is a part of marriage and that enjoyable sex does not always include orgasm. She does nothing to enhance their marriage by sharply decreasing the number of sexual intimacies.

Reflection Guide 14

1. Where will you go for your honeymoon?
2. What plans need to be made prior to the wedding?
3. Will you have privacy and adequate leisure?
4. Have you scheduled a doctor's examination? Have you a list of questions to ask him?
5. Should both use the same physician?
6. Will the physician deal with the virginal membrane if not already broken?
7. Do you know the various methods of conception control?
8. What method of birth control will you use on the honeymoon?
9. Do you desire children? How many? When do you plan for them to be born?
10. Do you have hereditary or physical or psychological apprehensions that make you fearful? Have you discussed them with your physician?

14

Preparation for the Honeymoon

Physical Examination

Forty of our fifty states require a health certificate before granting a couple a license to marry. Some require only serologic testing of the male; others specify medical examinations of both partners.

Visit the same physician, perhaps together and request more than a mere blood test to comply with the law. The wise couple has a complete medical, urological, and gynecological examination and a birth-control interview. If you see the doctor together, you should have a whole list of questions to ask, concerning such areas as birth-control methods, hereditary concerns, general health conditions, and sexual information. He can recommend any appropriate literature.

A systematic examination may reveal conditions that might affect your marital adjustment and require corrective measures. Explanations and assurances by the physician can give peace of mind to those with groundless apprehensions.

Dealing with Virginity

The hymen, a membrane tissue blocking access to the female vagina, sometimes is so rigid that the introduction of the male penis would cause some pain, ruining the bride's prospect of a pleasurable first night. Many gynecologists recommend that at least six weeks before marriage, if the membrane is still intact (which it may not be, even in virgins) and if tightness prevents the use of internal tampons for feminine hygiene, the bride should ask her doctor to break it surgically. This minor procedure lasts only minutes and takes place in his office.

Both bride and groom will benefit with a painless, pleasant initial sexual experience. It is unnecessary to endure the apprehension and burden of a sudden stretching or breaking of the hymen. Rupturing of the virginal membrane by the husband's penis generally causes slight bleeding. Blood loss is rarely dangerous and usually stops within a few minutes.

Birth-Control Methods

Birth control should be more accurately called conception control. Ideally parenthood results from a responsible act rather than an accident of physical union. Properly spaced pregnancies harm the health of neither mother nor child. The mother who has barely gotten over the strain of a previous birth has no vitality for another baby. Before the modern advances in birth control, many women suffered physical disability and mental anxiety because they had far too many babies. In my opinion, no prohibitive physical, psychological, or spiritual reason exists why birth control devices should not be used by newlyweds and other married people, including Christian people, who feel the need of expressing their love physically and yet who do not desire a baby conceived at this time.

There is no perfect birth-control method.

Diaphragm and Jelly

One of the safest and most widely used contraceptives is the diaphragm-and-jelly method. Individually fitted by a physician or at a clinic, a diaphragm is a rubber cap edged with a metal spring, which the woman places in the vagina. Jelly or cream, used with the diaphragm, aids in insertion and acts as a chemical barrier to sperm. She may insert it early, must leave the diaphragm in place for at least eight hours after intercourse, and does not need to douche with this method.

Birth-Control Pill

The most widely used and recently advanced contraceptive is the birth-control pill, which keeps egg cells from completely ripening. The tablets must be taken several weeks to establish their effect.

There are several advantages to the pill. It works quite reliably. In no way does it interfere with the enjoyment of sex. The wife takes care of everything, removing the fear of pregnancy.

The pill is not an unmixed blessing however. The tablets are purchased only by prescription. They alter natural body functions and may have harmful effects.

The Condom

Probably the best known and most widely used contraceptive is the condom. Readily available at drugstores, this method requires no special fitting or training in its use. The condom is a sheath that covers the male's penis, preventing sperm from entering the vagina. They are usually sold rolled; when ready for use, a small amount of vaginal jelly must be put on the tip of the condom, and it is rolled onto the penis, with additional lubricant added to the exterior. Most condoms are sufficiently thin and flexible, resulting in little loss of sensation. This method also has the advantage of protecting against venereal disease.

Considering these points, the condom may be the ideal contraceptive for newly marrieds.

Cream or Jelly Alone

Vaginal cream or jelly serves two purposes. The jelly acts as a barrier, closing off the opening of the cervix, and the chemicals in the jelly kill the male sperm. Some researchers claim this method as effective as the mechanical diaphragm.

Vaginal creams come with special applicators for insertion into the vagina. All the different types are easy to use, and they require no special training beyond the printed instructions that come with the package.

Suppositories that can be inserted into the vagina are also available. They melt about fifteen minutes after insertion, spreading a spermicidal agent throughout the area, to prevent pregnancy. Suppositories melt in hot weather, unless kept refrigerated, which precludes their use on spontaneous occasions outside your home.

The Rhythm Method

A woman's fertility lasts for only a very brief period following ovulation. If one could be certain just when ovulation took place, then "natural" conception control would be very simple. Unfortunately the procedure is quite complicated.

A woman ovulates around the middle of the menstrual cycle, that is, somewhere around the fourteenth day, if she has a twenty-eight day period. The ovum is impregnable for a very short time, estimated as between two and twelve hours. Sperm lasts only about forty-eight hours. So if a woman knew with certainty when she ovulated, control of conception would be no problem. The problem is that the menstrual cycles vary. Four-fifths of all women, it is estimated, vary five days or more in their cycles. The consensus of medical opinion is that the week preceding menstruation and a few days after are possibly the only safe period.[32]

Other Methods

Another type of contraceptive devise is the IUD. This device consists of a flexible piece of plastic or metal. When placed in the uterus by a doctor, it prevents pregnancy by keeping the fertilized egg from imbedding itself in the wall of the uterus.

Douches may also be used to wash out or kill the sperm cells before conception can take place, but they have little contraceptive value.

Other methods of conception control may be used sparingly with various degrees of risk. The most ancient method is withdrawal just before ejaculation, but it has its practical and psychological difficulties. Application of heat to the testicles has induced temporary sterility with no ill effect, but little data is available. Still in the laboratory stage is a vaccination in which the woman is injected with her husband's sperm; this sets up antibodies against that particular sperm. Some males are having vasectomies and some women have their fallopian tubes tied, thus making them sterile. In some cases, the operation can be reversed and fertilization recovered, but the percentage is quite low. The most unpopular method is abstinence.

The Honeymoon Place

When making plans for the honeymoon, you may choose a tourist area or a mutually enjoyable vacation locale. Privacy should be paramount in consideration; you will not want interruptions from family or friends. One fixed location is better than traveling all the time. Wherever you go, mutually agree upon the spot, considering the desires of both.

The honeymoon should last at least several days, so you can enjoy and explore each other in a relaxed, unhurried, and unscheduled atmosphere.

The destination for the first night of marriage should not be too far away in traveling time, so neither is too tired. Schedule the wedding sufficiently early in the day to allow early arrival at the first night's destination. After the tension and excitement of the marriage ceremony and reception, both bride and groom may be weary and not in the best condition for enjoying sex. If the husband immediately acts aggressively and demandingly, he may cause his bride pain and erect a barrier to and a distaste for intercourse. The bride may have some timidity and uncertainty at the inception of the new relationship. She needs to be courted and loved rather than forced. The husband should employ great gentleness and understanding. Actually, the marriage need not be consummated the first night at all if both feel too tired and keyed up. Perhaps getting a good night's sleep together, then pursuing the delights of sex the next day would be advisable. Whatever the case, preparation for sexual union is an artistry of playfulness and caressing, awakening the chords of passion and desire until each feels ready for complete participation. The honeymoon exists for the purpose of knowing each other intimately without the slightest fear or feelings of guilt and with special delight.

Reflection Guide 15

1. Do you know your state's waiting period regarding the marriage license?
2. Do you know the age requirements for marriage in your state?
3. Do you understand the law in making a marriage official?
4. Have you researched the legal rights of husbands and wives in your state?
5. What are the wife's property rights?
6. Can you name the three ways a marriage can be terminated?
7. Do you know the legal consequences of divorce?
8. Have you sufficiently prepared for your marriage so that it has a reasonably good chance of not being dissolved?
9. Are you both committed to doing your part to make your marriage work? Have both of you taken time to read this book thoroughly and to discuss the areas openly before proceeding?
10. Do you not agree it is better to remain unmarried than to be wrongly married? Is it better to be single and wish that you were married than to be married and wish that you were single again?

15

Marriage Laws

A great number of statutes control marriage, beginning before the wedding ceremony and continuing after the marriage ends. The law specifies the age below which you may not marry; it requires you to receive a license to marry and to take a premarital blood test for venereal disease. The wedding itself has legal sanctions; if you choose to have a civil ceremony, you are married by a representative of the state; if a clergyman marries you, he does so with legal power vested by state law. If you decide to terminate your marriage, you may do so only in ways specified by law.

Each state creates its own marriage and divorce laws. The requirement of a waiting period between the application for and issuance of a marriage license prevents hasty marriage. The period required before a divorce tends to encourage a couple to reconsider their life together. If a proposal of marriage is broken by one party, the other can sue, in some states, for breach of promise. In some states, special statutes provide for the return of engagement rings.

Who Can and Who Cannot Get Married

All but ten states require a waiting period of two to five days between the application for and granting of a marriage license or between issuance of the license and the ceremony. Exceptions are granted for persons who can show that waiting will pose special difficulties. These exceptions, however, do not lessen the law's discouragement of quick and easy marriages.

Every state specifies the minimum age of a prospective bride and groom. Most states require a blood test of each partner before issuing a license. If the tests indicate venereal disease, some states automatically deny the license, others grant it if the disease is in a nontransmittable stage.

All states forbid close blood relatives to marry; some states ban first cousins from marrying; many will not permit a woman to marry her brother-in-law or a man to marry his sister-in-law. Before 1967 interracial marriage was prohibited; since then there are no restrictions allowed in any state.

Common-Law Marriages

Thirteen states legally recognize common-law marriages (people living together, considering themselves husband and wife, without a marriage certificate or witnesses). The couple must be free of other marital ties, of legal age, sound mind, and acknowledge their status in some public fashion. In states that recognize common-law marriages, the woman may find it difficult to claim Social Security or veteran's benefits or to become heir to the man's estate.

The Marriage Ceremony

The overwhelming majority of Americans who marry are united in a civil or religious ceremony. Two essential elements legalize a marriage: the presence of witnesses (one of whom must be either a clergyman or a state official) and the declaration by the bride and groom of their intention to take each other as husband and wife for life. The law maintains flexibility regarding details or form of the ceremony.

Sample Application for Marriage License[33]

APPLICATION FOR MARRIAGE LICENSE, _____ COUNTY, TEXAS NO. _____

MALE

1 FULL NAME	FIRST	MIDDLE		LAST
2 SOCIAL SECURITY NUMBER	3 USUAL RESIDENCE	STREET NAME AND NUMBER	CITY	STATE
4 DATE OF BIRTH	5 PLACE OF BIRTH	CITY	COUNTY	STATE

6 PROOF OF IDENTITY AND AGE

7 IF DIVORCED, DID DIVORCE OCCUR WITHIN LAST 30 DAYS? YES ☐ NO ☐

8 I AM NOT PRESENTLY MARRIED TRUE ☐ FALSE ☐

9. The other applicant is not related to me as an ancestor or descendant by blood or adoption; a brother or sister, of the whole or half blood or by adoption; or a parent's brother or sister of the whole or half blood. True ☐ False ☐

FEMALE

10 FULL NAME	FIRST	MIDDLE	LAST	11 MAIDEN SURNAME
12 SOCIAL SECURITY NUMBER	13 USUAL RESIDENCE	STREET NAME AND NUMBER	CITY	STATE
14 DATE OF BIRTH	15 PLACE OF BIRTH	CITY	COUNTY	STATE

16 PROOF OF IDENTITY AND AGE

17. IF DIVORCED, DID DIVORCE OCCUR WITHIN LAST 30 DAYS? YES ☐ NO ☐

18 I AM NOT PRESENTLY MARRIED TRUE ☐ FALSE ☐

19. The other applicant is not related to me as an ancestor or descendant by blood or adoption; a brother or sister, of the whole or half blood or by adoption; or a parent's brother or sister of the whole or half blood. True ☐ False ☐

O A T H: I solemnly swear (or affirm) that the information I have given in this application is correct.

_____ _____
SIGNATURE OF THE MALE APPLICANT   SIGNATURE OF THE FEMALE APPLICANT

_____ _____ _____
NAME OF PERSON PERFORMING MARRIAGE   DATE OF MARRIAGE   COUNTY OF MARRIAGE

Mail Executed License to: _____ _____ _____
STREET ADDRESS   CITY, STATE, AND ZIP CODE

I certify that the applicant did not appear personally but the prerequisites for the license have been fulfilled as prescribed by Section 1.05 of the Family Code.

Subscribed and sworn to before me on _____, 19____

_____, 19____

_____ County Clerk
_____ County, Texas

By _____ Deputy

By _____

_____ County Clerk
_____ County, Texas

By _____ Deputy

LICENSE NO. _____ VOL. NO. _____ PAGE _____

Sample Marriage License[34]

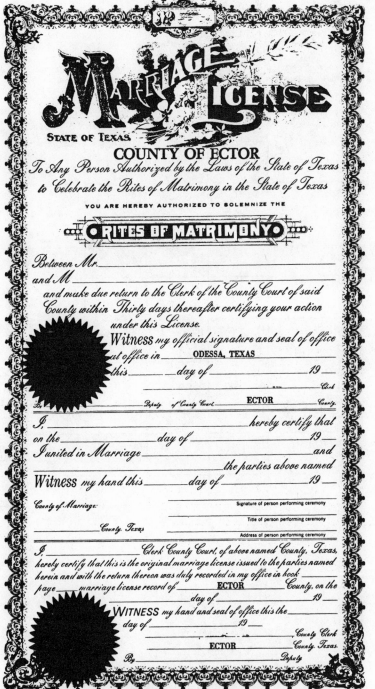

MARRIAGE LICENSE

STATE OF TEXAS

COUNTY OF ECTOR

To Any Person Authorized by the Laws of the State of Texas to Celebrate the Rites of Matrimony in the State of Texas

YOU ARE HEREBY AUTHORIZED TO SOLEMNIZE THE

···○ RITES OF MATRIMONY ○···

Between Mr._____

and M_____

and make due return to the Clerk of the County Court of said County within Thirty days thereafter certifying your action under this License.

Witness my official signature and seal of office at office in _____ ODESSA, TEXAS _____

this _____ day of _____ 19 ____

_____ Clerk

By ____ Deputy of County Court ____ ECTOR ____ County.

I, _____ hereby certify that on the _____ day of _____ 19 ____ I united in Marriage _____ and _____ the parties above named

Witness my hand this _____ day of _____ 19 ____

County of Marriage:

_____
Signature of person performing ceremony

_____
Title of person performing ceremony

_____ County, Texas _____
Address of person performing ceremony

I _____ Clerk County Court, of above named County, Texas, hereby certify that this is the original marriage license issued to the parties named herein and with the return thereon was duly recorded in my office in book ____ page ____ marriage license record of _____ ECTOR _____ County, on the _____ day of _____ 19 ____

WITNESS my hand and seal of office this the _____ day of _____ 19 ____

_____ County Clerk
ECTOR County, Texas.

By _____ Deputy

FORM 587 STAFFORD-LOWDON CO., FORT WORTH

MARRIAGE LAWS[35]

All states require that persons be at least a certain minimum age in order to obtain a marria cense. Persons below that age—18 in most states must usually have the consent of their pa under oath before a judge or a witness. Court approval may also be required. In all states, it is i for a man to marry his sister, half-sister, mother, daughter, granddaughter, grandmother, g grandmother, aunt, or niece. A woman may not marry her brother, half-brother, father,

| | At what age may you legally be married? | | | | What other re tives are you prohibited fro marrying?[1] |
| | With parental consent | | Without parental consent | | |
	Male	Female	Male	Female	
ALABAMA	14	14	18	18	Stepparent, st child, son-in-law, daughter law
ALASKA	16	16	18	18	——
ARIZONA	16	16	18	18	First cousin
ARKANSAS	17	16	21	18	First cousin
CALIFORNIA	No statutory provision	No statutory provision	18	18	——
COLORADO	16	16	18	18	——
CONNECTICUT	16	16	18	18	Stepparent, st child
DELAWARE	18	16	18	18	First cousin

[1] Besides siblings, parents, children, grandchildren, grandparents, great-grandparents, unc aunts, nieces, and nephews.

grandson, grandfather, great-grandfather, uncle, or nephew. Many states also prohibit marriages between more distant relatives. Every state must recognize a common-law marriage that has been entered into in another state and is considered valid in that state. These and other state laws regulating marriage are summarized below.

Is a blood test required to obtain a license?	What is the waiting period between application and issue of a license?	How soon after issue of license may you marry?	How long is license valid after issuance?	Are common-law marriages recognized?
Yes	None	Immediately	30 days	Yes
Yes	3 days	Immediately	90 days	No
Yes	None	Immediately	No statutory provision	No
Yes	3 days	Immediately	No statutory provision	No
Yes	None	Immediately	90 days	No
Yes	None	Immediately	30 days	Yes
Yes	4 days	Immediately	65 days	No
Yes	None	1 day[2]	30 days	No

[2] But there is a 4-day waiting period if both parties are nonresidents.

MARRIAGE LAWS[35] (continued)

	At what age may you legally be married?				What other re- tives are you prohibited fr marrying?[1]
	With parental consent		Without parental consent		
	Male	Female	Male	Female	
DISTRICT OF COLUMBIA	16	16	18	18	Stepparent, st child, stepgra parent, father law, mother-i law, son-in-la daughter-in-l spouse's gran parent or gra child, spouse grandparent grandchild
FLORIDA	16	16	18	18	—
GEORGIA	Under 16	Under 16	16	16	Stepparent, st child, step- grandparent, stepgrandchi father-in-law. mother-in-lav son-in-law, daughter-in-l
HAWAII	16	16	18	18	—
IDAHO	16	16	18	18	First cousin

Is a blood test required to obtain a license?	What is the waiting period between application and issue of a license?	How soon after issue of license may you marry?	How long is license valid after issuance?	Are common-law marriages recognized?
Yes	3 days	Immediately	No statutory provision	Yes
Yes	3 days	Immediately	30 days	No, unless entered into before Jan. 1, 1968
Yes	3 days	Immediately	30 days	Yes
Yes	None	Immediately	30 days	No
Yes	3 days if either is under 18; otherwise, none	Immediately	No statutory provision	Yes

MARRIAGE LAWS[35] (continued)

	At what age may you legally be married?				What other retives are you prohibited fro marrying?[1]
	With parental consent		Without parental consent		
	Male	Female	Male	Female	
ILLINOIS	16	16	18	18	First cousin
INDIANA	17	17	18	18	First cousin
IOWA	16	16	18	18	First cousin, stepparent, st child, father-law, mother-i law, son-in-la daughter-in-l spouse of gra child
KANSAS	Under 18	Under 18	18	18	First cousin
KENTUCKY	No statutory provision	No statutory provision	18	18	First cousin, cousin once r moved
LOUISIANA	18	16	18	18	First cousin
MAINE	16	16	18	18	Stepparent, st child, father-law, mother-i law, son-in-la daughter-in-l spouse's gran parent or gra child, spouse grandparent o grandchild

Is a blood test required to obtain a license?	What is the waiting period between application and issue of a license?	How soon after issue of license may you marry?	How long is license valid after issuance?	Are common-law marriages recognized?
Yes	None	3 days	60 days	No, unless entered into before June 30, 1905
Yes	3 days	Immediately	60 days	No, unless entered into before 1958
Yes	3 days	Immediately	20 days	Yes
Yes	3 days	Immediately	No statutory provision	Yes, but parties guilty of misdemeanor
Yes	3 days	Immediately	30 days	No
Yes	None	3 days	30 days	No
Yes	5 days	Immediately	60 days	No

MARRIAGE LAWS[35] *(continued)*

	At what age may you legally be married?				What other re‑
	With parental consent		Without parental consent		tives are you prohibited fro marrying?[1]
	Male	Female	Male	Female	
MARYLAND	16	16	18	18	Stepparent, s‑ child, father‑i law, mother‑i law, son‑in‑la daughter‑in‑l spouse's gran parent or grai child, spouse grandparent grandchild
MASSACHUSETTS	No statutory provision	No statutory provision	18	18	Stepparent, s‑ child, stepgra parent, father law, mother‑i law, son‑in‑la daughter‑in‑l
MICHIGAN	18	16	18	18	First cousin
MINNESOTA	No statutory provision	16	18	18	First cousin
MISSISSIPPI	—[3]	—[3]	17	15	First cousin, stepparent, st‑ child, father‑i law, mother‑i law, son‑in‑la daughter‑in‑l
MISSOURI	15	15	18	18	First cousin

[3] There is no statutory minimum age limit; both parental consent and court order are requi

Is a blood test required to obtain a license?	What is the waiting period between application and issue of a license?	How soon after issue of license may you marry?	How long is license valid after issuance?	Are common-law marriages recognized?
No	2 days	Immediately	6 months	No
Yes	3 days	Immediately	60 days	No
Yes	3 days	Immediately	33 days	No, unless entered into before Jan. 1, 1957
No	5 days	Immediately	6 months	No, unless entered into before Apr. 16, 1941
Yes	3 days if 1 person is under 21	Immediately	No statutory provision	No, unless entered into before Apr. 5, 1956
Yes	3 days	Immediately	No statutory provision	No, unless entered into before Mar. 31, 1921

MARRIAGE LAWS[35] (continued)

| | At what age may you legally be married? | | | | What other r... tives are you prohibited fr... marrying?[1] |
| | With parental consent | | Without parental consent | | |
	Male	Female	Male	Female	
MONTANA	16	16	18	18	First cousin
NEBRASKA	17	17	19	19	First cousin
NEVADA	16	16	18	18	First cousin
NEW HAMPSHIRE	14	13	18	18	First cousin, stepparent, so... in-law, daugh... in-law
NEW JERSEY	16	16	18	18	——
NEW MEXICO	16	16	18	18	——
NEW YORK	16	16	18	18	——
NORTH CAROLINA	16	16	18	18	Double first cousin
NORTH DAKOTA	16	16	18	18	First cousin

Is a blood test required to obtain a license?	What is the waiting period between application and issue of a license?	How soon after issue of license may you marry?	How long is license valid after issuance?	Are common-law marriages recognized?
Yes	None	3 days	180 days	Yes
Yes	2 days	Immediately	No statutory provision	No, unless entered into before 1923
No	None	Immediately	No statutory provision	No, unless entered into before Mar. 29, 1943
Yes	5 days	Immediately	90 days	No
Yes	3 days	Immediately	30 days	No, unless entered into before Dec. 1, 1939
Yes	None	Immediately	No statutory provision	No
Yes	None	1 day	60 days	No, unless entered into before Apr. 29, 1933
Yes[4]	None	Immediately	No statutory provision	No
Yes	None	Immediately	60 days	No

[4] A physical examination showing freedom from uncontrolled epilepsy, tuberculosis, idiocy, and insanity is also required.

MARRIAGE LAWS[35] *(continued)*

	At what age may you legally be married?				What other relatives are you prohibited from marrying?[1]
	With parental consent		Without parental consent		
	Male	Female	Male	Female	
OHIO	18	16	18	18	First cousin
OKLAHOMA	16	16	18	18	First cousin
OREGON	17	17	18	18	First cousin
PENNSYLVANIA	16	16	18	18	First cousin, stepparent, step child, son-in-law, daughter-law
RHODE ISLAND	18	16	18	18	Stepchild, father-in-law, mother-in-law, spouse's grand parent or grand child
SOUTH CAROLINA	16	14	18	18	Stepparent, step child, father-in law, mother-in law, son-in-law daughter-in-law spouse's grand parent or grand child, spouse's grandparent or grandchild
SOUTH DAKOTA	16	16	18	18	First cousin, stepparent, step child

Is a blood test required to obtain a license?	What is the waiting period between application and issue of a license?	How soon after issue of license may you marry?	How long is license valid after issuance?	Are common-law marriages recognized?
Yes	5 days	Immediately	60 days	Yes
Yes	3 days if either is under 18	Immediately	30 days	Yes
Yes	7 days	Immediately	30 days after blood test	No
Yes	3 days	Immediately	60 days	Yes
Yes	None[5]	Immediately	3 months	Yes
No	Yes	Immediately	No statutory provision	Yes
Yes	None	Immediately	20 days	No, unless entered into before July 1, 1959

[5] But there is a 5-day waiting period for female nonresidents.

MARRIAGE LAWS[35] (continued)

| | At what age may you legally be married? | | | | What other relatives are you prohibited from marrying?[1] |
| | With parental consent | | Without parental consent | | |
	Male	Female	Male	Female	
TENNESSEE	16	16	18	18	Stepparent, stepchild, stepgrandchild, grandnephew, grandniece
TEXAS	14	14	18	18	——
UTAH	14	14	18	18	First cousin
VERMONT	16	16	18	18	——
VIRGINIA	16	16	18	18	——
WASHINGTON	17	17	18	18	First cousin
WEST VIRGINIA	18	16	18	18	First cousin, double cousin
WISCONSIN	16	16	18	18	First cousin, unless female 55 years or older
WYOMING	16	16	18	18	First cousin

Is a blood test required to obtain a license?	What is the waiting period between application and issue of a license?	How soon after issue of license may you marry?	How long is license valid after issuance?	Are common-law marriages recognized?
Yes	3 days if either is under 18	Immediately	30 days	No
Yes[6]	None	Immediately	21 days after medical examination	Yes
Yes	None	Immediately	30 days	No
Yes	None	5 days from application of license	60 days	No
Yes	None	Immediately	60 days	No
No	3 days	Immediately	30 days	No
Yes	3 days	Immediately	60 days	No
Yes	5 days	Immediately	30 days	No, unless entered into before 1917
Yes	None	Immediately	No statutory provision	No

[6] A physical examination is also required.

Making a Marriage Official

Besides getting a marriage license, a bride and groom must see to it that proof of their marriage is put on file with the county clerk. After the ceremony, the clergyman or state official usually mails the marriage license to the county clerk for filing.

The Rights and Duties of Husbands and Wives

When major domestic difficulties arise, the law may step in to resolve them. A husband and wife are expected to live in the same house; under normal circumstances the husband has the legal right to decide where they shall live. If the husband's firm assigns him to a work in another part of the world, his wife has a legal duty to accompany him. If she refuses, she is guilty of desertion. The law is not inflexible: If her refusal is based upon health, she need not accompany her husband. A husband may not force his wife to a totally alien environment; in such a case he may be the one charged with desertion.

Wherever the home is located, the wife is the undisputed head. The husband cannot move his mother in and allow her to dominate the household. If she does, the wife can move out without a charge of desertion. The husband has no legal right to compel his wife to move in with his parents.

Supporting the Wife

The most fundamental law governing marriage is that a husband must support his wife. He must provide food, clothing, shelter, and medical care. If a husband refuses to do so and is not destitute himself, the wife may get a court order to force him to furnish these essentials.[36]

The courts conclude that however wealthy the husband, he

is not required to give his wife a luxurious existence, so long as the comforts he does provide are in keeping with the mode of life he has chosen.

The Right of Consortium

Between husband and wife there is no more important mutually enjoyed legal right than consortium, the conjugal relation of husband and wife. It gives one spouse the right to "the person, affection, society and assistance" of the other spouse.

A husband is as legally entitled to the domestic services of his wife as he is to her "affection and person." The husband need not pay her for performing the household tasks.

A husband may institute legal proceedings against any third party who, even inadvertently, deprives him of his wife's company and services. The law also recognizes the wife's equal right in this regard.

The Duties and Rights of a Working Wife

A husband has no claim on money his wife earns from outside-the-home employment. Under the law the paycheck belongs to her, to spend or save as she wishes.

A husband who owns a business can ask his wife to work for him without salary. However, he would be far wiser to pay her a salary. Should she be injured while working, unless she were a salaried employee, she could not collect disability payments under the Workmen's Compensation Act.

The Wife's Property

A wife has a right to own and control her own property acquired before marriage. In most states a woman also owns outright any property she acquires while married. However, in community-property states, all mutually acquired property belongs equally to husband and wife. A wife has the right "to make contracts, engage in business, be employed, keep outside earnings, and legal independence."[37] She can sue or be sued on her own. A husband is not liable for damage judgments against his wife, unless the harm done was partly his fault.

A wife's property remains beyond her husband's creditors. For this reason some husbands with large businesses vulnerable to damage suits transfer substantial family assets to their wives' ownership.

"A wife may convey her own property in any way she chooses, that is, she can sell it, leave it in a will, or give it to her children, family, friends, or charitable institutions."[38] She cannot turn it temporarily over to her husband and be sure of getting it back if he dies, unless she retains convincing evidence.

The Right Not to Have Children

"In 1965 the Supreme Court ruled that no state had the right to tell husbands and wives that they could not use artificial contraceptive devices; in every state, married people can now buy contraceptives, use them and obtain advice from doctors and clinics on the most suitable kinds"[39] without risking the danger of violating the law.

On January 22, 1973, the Supreme Court, in the landmark cases of *Roe* v. *Wade* and *Doe* v. *Balton,* held that a woman, after counsel with her doctor, has a constitutional right to make a decision to have an abortion. The medical definition of abortion is the termination of pregnancy prior to the stage of viability. She has the right to choose to continue a pregnancy or to end it.

The law states that abortion procedures must be performed by licensed physicians. In the first three months, abortion may be performed in a clinic or a doctor's office. After three months, special conditions may be imposed by certain states to protect and preserve the health of the woman. In the third trimester the state can regulate or prohibit all abortions except those necessary to protect a woman's life or health.[40]

"The ruling applies equally to all women, married and unmarried, adults and minors."[41]

Controversy still rages. Antiabortion activists have campaigned in Congress and throughout the states to reverse that decision by passing a constitutional amendment. Church bodies remain divided on the issue.

At present the legal situation is uniform: The law affirms the right of the woman to make her own decision regarding the continuation or termination of pregnancy.

Dissolving a Marriage

A couple can be legally parted in three ways: through annulment, legal separation, and divorce.

Annulment

An annulment is a court decision saying that some obstacle made the marriage invalid from the start. The law distinguishes two kinds of obstacles.

An incestuous marriage or a marriage contracted by a person who is already married automatically voids a marriage.

The following obstacles also form the basis for annulment:

UNDERAGE: "If either husband or wife was below the age for marriage set by law in their state, parents may bring legal action on behalf of their minor child."[42]

SEXUAL IMPOTENCE: "If either partner proves physically or psychologically incapable of intercourse from the beginning of the marriage, it can be annulled."[43]

LACK OF TRUE CONSENT: The validity of a marriage can be questioned if a couple gets married flippantly, with no real intention of a lasting relationship, if either is of unsound mind, or if either is married under duress.

FRAUD: Annulments have been granted for concealment of serious illness, mental disorder, important information about a previous marriage, pregnancy of a bride by a man other than her husband, lying by either partner about a desire to have children.

Legal Separations

When annulment is not possible, a divorce can end marriage. Couples who decide that they can no longer live together but who shy away from divorce may resort to the halfway step of a judicial separation. The proceeding requires one or both parties to appear in court, to negotiate the agreement; then they receive a decree of "divorce from bed and board."[44]

Separation does not entirely free a couple from responsibility of marriage. The husband is still obligated to support his wife and children and both husband and wife are barred from engaging in adulterous conduct, a difficult agreement to enforce.

If the couple reconciles after a voluntary separation, they simply tear up their agreement to live apart. In the case of a judicial separation, the court must be petitioned to revoke the agreement.

Divorce

The state laws provide a variety of grounds for legal divorce: physical cruelty, where one spouse inflicts bodily harm upon the other; mental cruelty, where one spouse persistently, with malicious intent, insults, abuses, or humiliates the other, making the marriage intolerable. Almost all states grant divorce for adultery, but only three recognize attempted murder of a spouse as grounds. Most states have adopted no-fault grounds for divorce; in such case a spouse no longer must prove that the other has committed a marital wrong.

There are four ways that divorce action can be stopped:

CONDONATION: If one has committed adultery but the spouse nevertheless allows the offender back home and they have intercourse, the forgiveness rules out the divorce for adultery suit.

CONNIVANCE: Where one spouse deliberately plots to create grounds for divorce against the other, a divorce will not be granted.

RECRIMINATION: If a husband and wife are equally guilty of misbehavior, neither can get a divorce.

COLLUSION: A couple conspiring to proffer false evidence will not receive a divorce.

Migratory Divorce

Some people become impatient with divorce proceedings so seek a quick release from unhappy marriages by obtaining migratory divorces in other countries or other states. Nevada, Idaho, Arkansas, South Dakota, and Wyoming have relaxed divorce laws, thus luring incoming divorce seekers. Residency requirements are six weeks in Nevada and Idaho, only sixty days in Wyoming and Arkansas, and none in South Dakota. The judge will usually hand down the divorce decree as soon as the residency requirements have been fulfilled. If the spouse does not consent to the divorce, but does not migrate to contest it, the judge gives the *ex parte* decree to the one appearing. A one-sided divorce bears the danger that such a decree may prove worthless if challenged in a court in the home state. If the spouse does cooperate, he or she signs an agreement that he or she recognizes and submits to the migratory divorce and will not later move to invalidate the decree.

Appendix

My Marriage Credo

I am thinking about marrying, Oh, my soul—what a thrilling adventure! What a decisive journey!

May I keep my head from being deluged by feelings and my heart passions from taking precedence over truth, so that an honest, objective appraisal can be made.

May I have the qualities of personality, the virtues of spirit, and the strength of character that will make me a lovable, loyal, and unselfish marriage partner.

May I learn to minimize weaknesses and be swift to praise the good.

May I never take another's love for granted, but always experience that breathless wonder that "out of all persons in the world, I have been chosen."

May I have enough success in my married life to expand opportunities for doing good for others, enough failure to keep my hands clenched in God's, enough tears to keep me tender, enough hurt to make me compassionate, enough faith to look to tomorrow.

I will give my very best to make my marriage a happy, enduring relationship as God intends and to heal the hurts with forgiveness.

When age and infirmity overtake me, and the sun begins to set on my life, may I have a mate who loves me still, clinging hand in hand together, and who at last will lay me to rest in the garden of God's dwelling.

Source Notes

1. William V. Thomas, *The Baltimore Sun*, 1982: reprinted in *The Odessa American*, 18 February 1982, p. 5A.

2. George R. Bach and Peter Wyden, *The Intimate Enemy: How to Fight Fair in Love and Marriage* (New York: William Morrow, 1969), p. 286.

3. Edward Carpenter, quoted in David R. Mace, *Whom God Hath Joined*, rev. ed. (Philadelphia: Westminster Press, 1973), p. 26.

4. F. Lofton Hudson, *'Till Divorce Us Do Part* (Nashville: Thomas B. Nelson, 1974), pp. 56, 57.

5. Robert Penske, "That Second Marriage Service: A Pastoral Worksheet," *Journal of Pastoral Care*, March 1974, p. 17.

6. Jim Smoke, *Growing Through Divorce* (Eugene, Oreg.: Harvest House, 1974), p. 112.

7. Aaron Rutledge, *Premarital Counseling* (Cambridge, Mass.: Schenkman, 1966), p. 25.

8. Charlie W. Shedd, *Letters to Karen* (Old Tappan, N.J.: Fleming H. Revell, 1965), p. 19.

9. H. J. Clinebell, Jr., "Philosophical-Religious Factors in the Etiology and Treatment of Alcoholism," *Quarterly Journal of Studies on Alcohol* 24, no. 3 (September 1963), p. 477.

10. Fulton Sheen, *Three to Get Married* (New York: Dell, 1951), p. 13.

11. Ibid., p. 12.

12. Ibid., p. 14.

13. Abigail Van Buren, "Dear Abby," *The Odessa American*, 27 February 1982.

14. *Pre-Marital Counseling Guide,* (Philadelphia: Fortress Press).

15. Elizabeth Achtemeier, *The Committed Marriage* (Philadelphia: Westminster Press, 1976), p. 77.

16. Ibid., p. 178.

17. Harold Ivan Smith, *Single Life in a Double Bed* (Eugene, Oreg.: Harvest House, 1979), p. 79.

18. Ibid., p. 80.

19. Form used by James L. Christensen, Odessa, Texas.

20. James L. Christensen, *The Ministers' Wedding Handbook* (Old Tappan, N.J.: Fleming H. Revell, 1963), pp. 21, 22.

21. Natalia M. Belting and James R. Hine, *Your Wedding Workbook* (Danville, Ill.: Interstate, 1977), p. 22.

22. Achtemeier, *The Committed Marriage*, p. 40.

23. Kenneth H. Foreman, *From This Day Forward: Thoughts About Christian Marriage* (Richmond, Va.: Outlook, 1950), p. 16.

24. Tim and Beverly LaHaye, *The Act of Marriage* (Grand Rapids, Mich.: Zondervan, 1976), p. 11.

25. Charlotte H. Clinebell and Howard J. Clinebell, Jr., *The Intimate Marriage* (New York: Harper & Row, 1970), pp. 136–139.

26. W. Clark Ellzery, *How to Keep Romance in Your Marriage* (New York: Associated Press, 1954), p. 171.

27. Reuel Howe, "The Pastor Speaks of Sex and Marriage," *Reader's Digest,* October 1958, p. 78.

28. Edrita Fried, *The Ego in Love and Sexuality* (New York: Grune and Stratton, 1960), p. 1.

29. Clinebell, *The Intimate Marriage*, p. 38.

30. Ibid., p. 36.

31. S. A. Lewin and John Gilmore, *Sex Without Fear* (New York: Medical Research Press, 1951), p. 38.

32. Ibid.

33. State of Texas, application for marriage license.

34. Ector County, Texas, sample marriage license.

35. Inge N. Dobelis, ed., *Reader's Family Legal Guide* (Pleasantville, N.Y.: Reader's Digest, 1981), pp. 1130–1135.

36. David S. Thompson, "The Family," in *The Time-Life Family Legal Guide,* ed. John Dille (New York: Time-Life Books, 1971), p. 64.

37. Ibid., p. 67.

38. Ibid., p. 68.

39. Ibid., p. 69.

40. Pregnancy Resource Books, *Deciding on Abortion* (New York: Planned Parenthood Federation of America, 1981).

41. Marjory Skowronski, *Abortion and Alternatives* (Millbrae, Calif.: Les Femmes Pubs., 1977), p. 1.

42. Thompson, "The Family," p. 50.

43. Ibid.

44. Ibid., p. 51.

Recommended Reading

Achtemeier, Elizabeth. *The Committed Marriage*. Philadelphia: Westminster Press, 1976.

Berther, Ruth and Edward. *An Analysis of Human Sexual Response: The Masters and Johnson Study*. New York: Signet, 1966.

Clinebell, Charlotte H. and Clinebell, Howard J., Jr. *The Intimate Marriage*. New York: Harper & Row, 1970.

Capon, Robert F. *Bed and Board: Plain Talk About Marriage*. New York: Simon and Schuster, 1965.

Cleveland, McDonald. *Creating a Successful Christian Marriage*. Grand Rapids, Mich.: Baker Book House, 1975.

Collins, Gary R. *Christian Counseling*. Waco, Tex.: Word Books, 1980.

Crane, George W. *Tests for Sweethearts*. Chicago: Hopkins Syndicate, 1956.

Denton, Wallace. *Family Problems and What to Do About Them*. Philadelphia: Westminster Press, 1971.

Dille, John, ed. *The Time-Life Family Legal Guide*. New York: Time-Life Books, 1971.

Duvall, Evelyn M. *The Art of Dating*. New York: Permabooks, 1958.

161

Duvall, Evelyn M. *Why Wait Till Marriage.* New York: Association Press, 1965.

Duvall, Evelyn M. *When You Marry.* New York: Association Press, 1953.

Eichenlaub, John E. *The Marriage Art.* New York: Dell, 1979.

Flach, Frederic F. *A New Marriage, A New Life.* New York: McGraw-Hill, 1978.

Foreman, Kenneth H. *From This Day Forward: Thoughts About Christian Marriage.* Richmond, Va.: Outlook, 1950.

Fromm, Erich. *The Art of Loving: An Enquiry Into the Nature of Love.* New York: Harper & Row, 1956.

Greenblat, Bernard R. *A Doctor's Marital Guide for Patients.* Chicago: Budlong Press, 1964.

Howe, Reuel L. *Herein Is Love.* Valley Forge, Pa.: Judson Press, 1961.

LaHaye, Tim. *Understanding the Male Temperament.* Old Tappan, N.J.: Fleming H. Revell, 1977.

LaHaye, Tim and Beverly. *The Act of Marriage.* Grand Rapids, Mich.: Zondervan. 1976.

Lewin, S. A. and Gilmore, John. *Sex Without Fear.* New York: Medical Research Press, 1951.

Mace, David. *Success in Marriage.* Nashville, Tenn.: Abingdon, 1958.

Mace, David R. *Whom God Hath Joined.* Rev. ed. Philadelphia: Westminster Press, 1973.

Mace, David R. and Mace, Vera. *We Can Have Better Marriages if We Really Want Them.* Nashville, Tenn.: Abingdon, 1974.

McGinnis, Tom. *Your First Year of Marriage.* New York: Doubleday, 1967.

McHugh, Gelolo. *Marriage Counselor's Manual and Teacher's Handbook for Use With the Sex Knowledge Inventory.* Durham, N.C.: Family Life Publications, 1968.

Smith, Harold Ivan. *Single Life in a Double Bed.* Eugene, Oreg.: Harvest House, 1979.

Thompson, David A. *A Premarital Guide for Couples and Their Counselors.* Minneapolis: Bethany House, 1979.

Tournier, Paul. *To Understand Each Other.* Richmond, Va.: John Knox Press, 1967.

Trueblood, Elton. *Common Ventures of Life.* New York: Harper & Brothers, n.d.

Trueblood, Elton. *The Recovery of Family Life.* New York: Harper & Brothers, 1953.

Wood, Leland Foster. *Harmony in Marriage.* Old Tappan, N.J.: Fleming H. Revell, 1979.

Wright, Norman H. *Communication: Key to Your Marriage.* Glendale, Calif.: Regal, 1974.